MUNRO BAGGING

LOG BOOK & Photobook

Scotland's Munros, a list of Scottish mountains which are named after
Sir Hugh T Munro, who surveyed and cataloged them in 1891.
Climbing these peaks is a great way for experienced walkers to explore some
of Scotland's finest scenery and further-flung locations.

Munro bagging is a popular pastime in Scotland where walking enthusiasts
challenge themselves to climb as many of the peaks as they can - over 6,000
people, called 'compleatists' have climbed them all so far. If you're wondering
about the spelling above, it's archaic, though we think a cute version of
'complete', which all adds to the tradition of the pursuit.
It's also a pastime to savor, however, if you're a mountain goat and want to
challenge the quickest round record, set by Munroist Stephen Pyke in 2010,
you'll have just 39 days, 9 hours, and 6 minutes!

It is always important to be safe when exploring Scotland's mountains and
rugged landscapes.
Bringing the correct equipment, wearing appropriate clothing and footwear,
and educating yourself about the environment around you is key for ensuring
your safety.

Author message:

After 2 months of continuous work, I finished this logbook, I tried in this
logbook to cover all the information that every bagger needs to record with
a place of a picture of you and your companions in every Munro,
which is new and exclusive.
I hope it helps you to record your achievements and memorable moments
along the way.
I want to thank you for your purchase. actually, I would really appreciate
a review from you, it will motivate me to make more and create more.
I also looking for your feedback, I definitely want to hear from you if you think
that something needed to improve in this logbook, so be sure to email me
«SABRAPRINTSB@GMAIL.COM» and I will see what I can do.

CHECKLIST

PAGE CHEKING	MUNRO	PAGE CHEKING	MUNRO
1	BEINN TEALLACH	35	MEALL BUIDHE
2	CARN AOSDA	36	BEINN CHABHAIR
3	BEN VANE	37	THE CAIRNWELL
4	BEINN A' CHLEIBH	38	MAOL CHEAN-DEARG
5	MEALL NA TEANGA	39	FIONN BHEINN
6	GEAL-CHARN	40	BEINN TARSUINN
7	CREAG NAN DAMH	41	MEALL A' CHRASGAIDH
8	A' GHLAS-BHEINN	42	AM BASTEIR
9	SGURR A' MHADAIDH	43	BEINN NA LAP
10	RUADH STAC MOR	44	A' BHUIDHEANACH BHEAG
11	GAIRICH	45	BEINN SGULAIRD
12	SGIATH CHUIL	46	SRON A' CHOIRE GHAIRBH
13	CARN SGULAIN	47	MOUNT KEEN
14	AN SOCACH	48	LUINNE BHEINN
15	BEINN ALLIGIN - TOM NA GRUAGAICH	49	MULLACH NAN COIREAN
16	SGURR NAN EACH	50	CARN NA CAIM
17	CREAG PITRIDH	51	CARN DEARG
18	AN COILEACHAN	52	BEINN A' CHROIN
19	BUACHAILLE ETIVE BEAG - STOB COIRE RAINEACH	53	BEN VORLICH
20	MEALL A' CHOIRE LEITH	54	BINNEIN BEAG
21	GEAL CHARN	55	AN SOCACH
22	BEINN LIATH MHOR	56	SGURR DUBH MOR
23	SEANA BHRAIGH	57	STOB A' CHOIRE ODHAIR
24	SGURR NAN EAG	58	BIDEIN A' CHOIRE SHEASGAICH
25	BEINN NARNAIN	59	CARN BHAC
26	EIDIDH NAN CLACH GEALA	60	CARN DEARG
27	BEN HOPE	61	BEINN TULAICHEAN
28	MEALL NAN EUN	62	CREAG A' MHAIM
29	MAYAR	63	SGURR NA SGINE
30	MORUISG	64	MEALL BUIDHE
31	BLA BHEINN	65	DRIESH
32	A' CHAILLEACH	66	SGURR MHIC CHOINNICH
33	BEN CHONZIE	67	BEINN BHUIDHE
34	BEINN BHREAC	68	MEALL GORM

#	Name	#	Name
69	MEALL CHUAICH	106	MEALL NAN CEAPRAICHEAN
70	AONACH EAGACH - MEALL DEARG	107	BEINN DUBHCHRAIG
71	BEINN MHANACH	108	CONA' MHEALL
72	AM FAOCHAGACH	109	STOB COIRE SGRIODAIN
73	BUACHAILLE ETIVE MOR - STOB NA BROIGE	110	BEINN A' CHOCHUILL
74	SGURR NAN COIREACHAN	111	MAOL CHINN-DEARG
75	BEINN LIATH MHOR FANNAICH	112	MEALL NA AIGHEAN
76	SGOR GAIBHRE	113	SLIOCH
77	SGURR NAN COIREACHAN	114	CISTE DHUBH
78	SAILEAG	115	STOB COIRE A' CHAIRN
79	TOM BUIDHE	116	AN GEARANACH
80	CARN GHLUASAID	117	MULLACH NA DHEIRAGAIN
81	BUACHAILLE ETIVE BEAG - STOB DUBH	118	BEN VORLICH
82	TOLMOUNT	119	SGURR DEARG
83	BRUACH NA FRITHE	120	BEINN ALLIGIN - SGÙRR MHOR
84	MEALL GLAS	121	DRUIM SHIONNACH
85	BEINN FHIONNLAIDH	122	GAOR BHEINN (GULVAIN)
86	STUCHD AN LOCHAIN	123	LURG MHOR
87	BEINN NAN AIGHENAN	124	CONIVAL
88	SGORR RUADH	125	CREAG LEACACH
89	BEN KLIBRECK	126	BEINN EUNAICH
90	SGURR THUILM	127	SGURR BAN
91	CARN A' CHLAMAIN	128	SGAIRNEACH MHOR
92	SGURR NA BANACHDICH	129	CARN NAN GOBHAR
93	BEN MORE	130	SGURR ALASDAIR
94	SGURR NAN GILLEAN	131	SGURR NA RUAIDHE
95	A' MHAIGHDEAN	132	CARN NAN GOBHAR
96	AONACH EAGACH - SGORR NAM FIANNAIDH	133	BEINN EIGHE - SPIDEAN COIRE NAN CLACH
97	MEALL GARBH	134	CARN AN FHIDHLEIR
98	SGURR A' GHREADAIDH	135	SGURR NA H-ULAIDH
99	A' MHARCONAICH	136	AN CAISTEAL
100	BEN LOMOND (BEINN LAOMAINN)	137	SPIDEAN MIALACH
101	BEINN SGRITHEALL	138	A' CHAILLEACH
102	STUC A' CHROIN	139	GLAS BHEINN MHOR
103	CARN A' GHEOIDH	140	BROAD CAIRN
104	BEINN A' GHLO - CÀRN LIATH	141	BEN MORE ASSYNT
105	STOB BAN	142	SGURR BREAC

143	SAIL CHAORAINN	180		BEN OSS
144	STOB DAIMH	181		CARN GORM
145	SGURR CHOINNICH	182		CARN ANRIGH
146	STOB BAN	183		AM BODACH
147	MEALL GREIGH	184		BEINN FHADA
148	BEINN A' BHEITHIR - SGORR DHONUILL	185		CARN DEARG
149	AONACH MEADHOIN	186		GLEOURAICH
150	SGURR NA CARNACH	187		SGURR A' BHEALAICH DHEIRG
151	SGURR MOR	188		CARN A' MHAIM
152	BEINN AN DOTHAIDH	189		BEINN ACHALADAIR
153	SGURR AN LOCHAIN	190		MEALL GHAORDAIDH
154	BEINN FHIONNLAIDH	191		SGURR NA CICHE
155	MAOILE LUNNDAIDH	192		CARN MAIRG
156	CARN LIATH	193		MEALL NAN TARMACHAN
157	AN SGARSOCH	194		STOB COIR'AN ALBANNAICH
158	THE DEVIL'S POINT	195		BEINN IUTHARN MHOR
159	BEINN DEARG	196		CRUACH ARDRAIN
160	SGURR EILDE MOR	197		CHNO DEARG
161	SGURR AN DOIRE LEATHAIN	198		BEN WYVIS
162	BEINN EIGHE - RUADH-STAC MOR	199		CREAG MHOR
163	BEINN UDLAMAIN	200		CàRN AN T-SAGAIRT MOR
164	THE SADDLE	201		GEAL CHARN
165	CAIRN BANNOCH	202		SGURR FHUAR-THUILL
166	BEINN IME	203		BEINN A' CHAORAINN
167	GARBH CHIOCH MHOR	204		GLAS TULAICHEAN
168	MULLACH COIRE MHIC FHEARCHAIR	205		SGURR A' CHAORACHAIN
169	BEINN BHEOIL	206		STOB POITE COIRE ARDAIR
170	CARN AN TUIRC	207		TOLL CREAGACH
171	MULLACH CLACH A' BHLAIR	208		NA GRUAGAICHEAN
172	AONACH AIR CHRITH	209		LIATHACH
173	LADHAR BHEINN	210		AN TEALLACH - SGURR FIONA
174	BUACHAILLE ETIVE MOR - STOB DEARG	211		AN TEALLACH - BIDEIN A' GHLAS THUILL
175	LIATHACH - MULLACH AN RATHAIN	212		CAIRN OF CLAISE
176	BEINN A' BHEITHIR - SGORR DHEARG	213		GLAS MAOL
177	BEN CHALLUM	214		SGURR FHUARAN
178	SGURR A' MHAORAICH	215		MEALL CORRANAICH
179	SGURR NA CISTE DUIBHE	216		AN SOCACH

#	Name	#	Name
217	BEINN A' GHLO - BRAIGH COIRE CHRUINN-BHALGAIN	250	AN RIABHACHAN
218	BIDEAN NAM BIAN - STOB COIRE SGREAMHACH	251	BEINN A' GHLO - CARN NAN GABHAR
219	BEINN DORAIN	252	MEALL GARBH
220	BEINN HEASGARNICH	253	BEN CRUACHAN
221	BEN STARAV	254	CREAG MEAGAIDH
222	BEINN A' CHREACHAIN	255	BEN LUI
223	SCHIEHALLION	256	BINNEIN MOR
224	BEINN A' CHAORAINN	257	GEAL-CHARN
225	SGURR A' CHOIRE GHLAIS	258	BEN ALDER
226	BEINN DEARG	259	BIDEAN NAM BIAN
227	BEINN A' CHLACHAIR	260	SGURR NAN CEATHREAMHNAN
228	STOB GHABHAR	261	SGURR NA LAPAICH
229	BYNACK MORE	262	DERRY CAIRNGORM
230	SGURR NAN CLACH GEALA	263	LOCHNAGAR
231	SGURR CHOINNICH MòR	264	BEINN BHROTAIN
232	SGURR A' MHAIM	265	STOB BINNEIN
233	CREISE	266	BEN AVON
234	MULLACH FRAOCH-CHOIRE	267	BEN MORE
235	BEINN GHLAS	268	MUNSTOB CHOIRE CLAURIGHRO
236	BEINN EIBHINN	269	MAM SODHAIL
237	STOB A' CHOIRE MHEADHOIN	270	CARN EIGE
238	MEALL A' BHUIRIDH	271	BEINN MHEADHOIN
239	SGURR MOR	272	BEINN A' BHUIRD
240	SGURR NAN CONBHAIREAN	273	BEN LAWERS
241	CARN A' CHOIRE BHOIDHEACH	274	CARN MOR DEARG
242	TOM A' CHOINICH	275	AONACH MOR
243	MONADH MOR	276	AONACH BEAG
244	STOB COIRE EASAIN	277	CAIRN GORM
245	AONACH BEAG	278	SGOR AN LOCHAIN UAINE
246	STOB COIRE AN LAOIGH	279	CAIRN TOUL
247	AN STUC	280	BRAERIACH
248	SGOR GAOITH	281	BEN MACDUI
249	A' CHRAILEAG	282	BEN NEVIS

BEINN TEALLACH

Region	Area	Height
Loch Lochy to Loch Laggan	Highland	914.6 M / 3001 FEET

Date: .... Munro order: ....

Duration: .... Summit time: ....

Distance covered: .... Start time: ___:___   Finish time: ___:___

Companions: ....
....

— Weather condition: —   — Rating —

Difficulty: ☆☆☆☆☆
Relish: ☆☆☆☆☆
Memories: ☆☆☆☆☆

Notes: ....
....

CARN AOSDA

Region	Area	Height
Pitlochry to Braemar & Blairgowrie	Aberdeenshire	915.3 M / 3003 FEET

Date: .... Munro order: ....

Duration: .... Summit time: ....

Distance covered: .... Start time: ___:___   Finish time: ___:___

Companions: ....
....

— Weather condition: —

☀ ⛅ ☁ 🌧 ⛈ 🌨

— Rating —

Difficulty: ☆ ☆ ☆ ☆ ☆

Relish: ☆ ☆ ☆ ☆ ☆

Memories: ☆ ☆ ☆ ☆ ☆

Notes: ....
....

BEN VANE

Region	Area	Height
Inveraray to Crianlarich	Agryll and Bute	915.76 M / 3004 FEET

Date: .... Munro order: ....

Duration: .... Summit time: ....

Distance covered: .... Start time: ___:___   Finish time: ___:___

Companions: ....

....

— Weather condition: —

☐ ☀ ☐ ⛅ ☐ ☁ ☐ 🌧 ☐ ⛈ ☐ 🌨

— Rating —

Difficulty: ☆ ☆ ☆ ☆ ☆

Relish: ☆ ☆ ☆ ☆ ☆

Memories: ☆ ☆ ☆ ☆ ☆

Notes: ....

....

BEINN A' CHLEIBH

Region	Area	Height
Inveraray to Crianlarich	Argyll and Bute /Stirling	916.3 M /3006 FEET

Date: .... Munro order: ....

Duration: .... Summit time: ....

Distance covered: .... Start time: ___:___   Finish time: ___:___

Companions: ....
....

— Weather condition: —   — Rating —

☐ ☀ ☐ ⛅ ☐ 🌥 ☐ 🌧 ☐ ⛈ ☐ 🌨

Difficulty: ☆☆☆☆☆
Relish: ☆☆☆☆☆
Memories: ☆☆☆☆☆

Notes: ....
....

MEALL NA TEANGA

Region	Area	Height
Loch Arkaig to Glen Moriston	Highland	916.8 M / 3008 FEET

Date: .... Munro order: ....

Duration: .... Summit time: ....

Distance covered: .... Start time: ___:___   Finish time: ___:___

Companions: ....

....

....

――― Weather condition: ―――

☐ ☀ ☐ ⛅ ☐ ☁ ☐ 🌧 ☐ ⛈ ☐ 🌨

――― Rating ―――

Difficulty: ☆ ☆ ☆ ☆ ☆

Relish: ☆ ☆ ☆ ☆ ☆

Memories: ☆ ☆ ☆ ☆ ☆

PICTURE HERE

Notes: ....

....

GEAL CHARN

Region	Area	Height
Loch Ericht to Glen Tromie & Glen Garry	Highland	917.1 M / 3009 FEET

Date: .... Munro order: ....

Duration: .... Summit time: ....

Distance covered: .... Start time: ___:___   Finish time: ___:___

Companions: ....

....

— Weather condition: —

☐ ☀ ☐ ⛅ ☐ ☁ ☐ 🌧 ☐ ⛈ ☐ 🌨

— Rating —

Difficulty: ☆ ☆ ☆ ☆ ☆

Relish: ☆ ☆ ☆ ☆ ☆

Memories: ☆ ☆ ☆ ☆ ☆

Notes: ....
....

CREAG NAN DAMH

Region	Area	Height
Glen Shiel to Loch Hourn and Loch Quoich	Highland	917.2 M / 3012 FEET

Date: .... Munro order: ....

Duration: .... Summit time: ....

Distance covered: .... Start time: ___:___   Finish time: ___:___

Companions: ....

....

....

— Weather condition: —

☐ ☀ ☐ ⛅ ☐ 🌥 ☐ 🌧 ☐ ⛈ ☐ 🌨

— Rating —

Difficulty: ☆ ☆ ☆ ☆ ☆

Relish: ☆ ☆ ☆ ☆ ☆

Memories: ☆ ☆ ☆ ☆ ☆

PICTURE HERE

Notes: ....

....

A' GHLAS-BHEINN

Region	Area	Height
Loch Duich to Cannich	Highland	918 M /3012 FEET

Date: .... Munro order: ....

Duration: .... Summit time: ....

Distance covered: .... Start time: ___:___   Finish time: ___:___

Companions: ....

─── Rating ───

Difficulty: ☆ ☆ ☆ ☆ ☆

Relish: ☆ ☆ ☆ ☆ ☆

Memories: ☆ ☆ ☆ ☆ ☆

─── Weather condition: ───

☐ ☀ ☐ ⛅ ☐ ☁ ☐ 🌧 ☐ ⛈ ☐ 🌨

Notes: ....
....

SGURR A' MHADAIDH

Region	Area	Height
Minginish and the Cuillin Hills	Highland	918 M / 3012 FEET

Date: .... Munro order: ....

Duration: .... Summit time: ....

Distance covered: .... Start time: ___:___   Finish time: ___:___

Companions: ....

....

—— Weather condition: —— ———— Rating ————

☀ ⛅ ☁ 🌧 ⛈ 🌨

Difficulty: ☆☆☆☆☆

Relish: ☆☆☆☆☆

Memories: ☆☆☆☆☆

PICTURE HERE

Notes: ....
....

RUADH STAC MOR

Region	Area	Height
Loch Maree to Loch Broom	Highland	918.7 M / 3014 FEET

Date: ....

Munro order: ....

Duration: ....

Summit time: ....

Distance covered: ....

Start time: ___:___   Finish time: ___:___

Companions: ....
....

— Rating —

Difficulty: ☆ ☆ ☆ ☆ ☆

Relish: ☆ ☆ ☆ ☆ ☆

Memories: ☆ ☆ ☆ ☆ ☆

— Weather condition: —

☐ ☀ ☐ ⛅ ☐ ☁ ☐ 🌧 ☐ ⛈ ☐ 🌨

PICTURE HERE

Notes: ....
....

GAIRICH

Region	Area	Height
Knoydart to Glen Kingie	Highland	919 M /3015 FEET

Date: .... Munro order: ....

Duration: .... Summit time: ....

Distance covered: .... Start time: ___:___   Finish time: ___:___

Companions: ....

....

— Weather condition: —

☀ 🌤 ☁ 🌧 ⛈ 🌨

— Rating —

Difficulty: ☆ ☆ ☆ ☆ ☆

Relish: ☆ ☆ ☆ ☆ ☆

Memories: ☆ ☆ ☆ ☆ ☆

Notes: ....

....

SGIATH CHUIL

Region	Area	Height
Glen Lyon to Glen Dochart & Loch Tay	Stirling	920.1 M /3019 FEET

Date: .... Munro order: ....

Duration: .... Summit time: ....

Distance covered: .... Start time: ___:___   Finish time: ___:___

Companions: ....

....

Weather condition:
☐ ☀ ☐ ⛅ ☐ ☁ ☐ 🌧 ☐ ⛈ ☐ 🌨

Rating
Difficulty: ☆☆☆☆☆
Relish: ☆☆☆☆☆
Memories: ☆☆☆☆☆

Notes: ....

....

CARN SGULAIN

Region	Area	Height
Glen Albyn and the Monadh Liath	Highland	920.3 M / 3019 FEET

Date: .... Munro order: ....

Duration: .... Summit time: ....

Distance covered: .... Start time: ___:___   Finish time: ___:___

Companions: ....
....
....

Weather condition:
☐ ☀ ☐ ⛅ ☐ ☁ ☐ 🌧 ☐ ⛈ ☐ 🌨

Rating
Difficulty: ☆☆☆☆☆
Relish: ☆☆☆☆☆
Memories: ☆☆☆☆☆

Notes: ....
....

AN SOCACH

Region	Area	Height
Loch Duich to Cannich	Highland	921 M / 3022 FEET

Date: .... Munro order: ....

Duration: .... Summit time: ....

Distance covered: .... Start time: ___:___   Finish time: ___:___

Companions: ....

— Weather condition: —

— Rating —

Difficulty: ☆☆☆☆☆
Relish: ☆☆☆☆☆
Memories: ☆☆☆☆☆

Notes: ....

BEINN ALLIGIN
TOM NA GRUAGAICH

Region	Area	Height
Loch Torridon to Loch Maree	Highland	922 M / 3025 FEET

Date: .... Munro order: ....

Duration: .... Summit time: ....

Distance covered: .... Start time: ___:___   Finish time: ___:___

Companions: ....

....

— Weather condition: — ——— Rating ———

☐ ☀ ☐ ⛅ ☐ ☁ ☐ 🌧 ☐ ⛈ ☐ 🌨

Difficulty: ☆ ☆ ☆ ☆ ☆
Relish: ☆ ☆ ☆ ☆ ☆
Memories: ☆ ☆ ☆ ☆ ☆

Notes: ....

....

SGURR NAN EACH

Region	Area	Height
Loch Rannoch to Glen Lyon	Perth and Kinross	923 M /3028 FEET

Date: .... Munro order: ....

Duration: .... Summit time: ....

Distance covered: .... Start time: ___:___   Finish time: ___:___

Companions: ....

Rating

Difficulty: ☆☆☆☆☆

Relish: ☆☆☆☆☆

Memories: ☆☆☆☆☆

Weather condition: ☀ ⛅ ☁ 🌧 ⛈ 🌨

Notes: ....

AN COILEACHAN

Region	Area	Height
The Fannaichs	Highland	923.9 M / 3031 FEET

Date: ....   Munro order: ....

Duration: ....   Summit time: ....

Distance covered: ....   Start time: ___:___   Finish time: ___:___

Companions: ....
....
....

— Weather condition: —

— Rating —

Difficulty: ☆☆☆☆☆

Relish: ☆☆☆☆☆

Memories: ☆☆☆☆☆

PICTURE HERE

Notes: ....
....

CREAG PITRIDH

Region	Area	Height
Loch Treig to Loch Ericht	Highland	924 M / 3031 FEET

Date: .... Munro order: ....

Duration: .... Summit time: ....

Distance covered: .... Start time: ___:___   Finish time: ___:___

Companions: ....

....

Weather condition: ☀ ⛅ ☁ 🌧 ⛈ 🌨

Rating
Difficulty: ☆☆☆☆☆
Relish: ☆☆☆☆☆
Memories: ☆☆☆☆☆

Notes: ....

....

BUACHAILLE ETIVE BEAG
STOB COIRE RAINEACH

Region	Area	Height
Loch Linnhe to Loch Etive	Highland	925 M / 3035 FEET

Date: .... Munro order: ....

Duration: .... Summit time: ....

Distance covered: .... Start time: ___:___   Finish time: ___:___

Companions: ....
....
....

Weather condition:
☀ ⛅ 🌥 🌧 ⛈ 🌨

Rating
Difficulty: ☆☆☆☆☆
Relish: ☆☆☆☆☆
Memories: ☆☆☆☆☆

PICTURE HERE

Notes: ....
....

MEALL A' CHOIRE LEITH

Region	Area	Height
Glen Lyon to Glen Do-chart & Loch Tay	Perth and Kinross	925.6 M / 3037 FEET

Date: .... Munro order: ....

Duration: .... Summit time: ....

Distance covered: .... Start time: ___:___   Finish time: ___:___

Companions: ....

— Weather condition: —   — Rating —

☀ ⛅ ☁ 🌧 ⛈ 🌨

Difficulty: ☆☆☆☆☆
Relish: ☆☆☆☆☆
Memories: ☆☆☆☆☆

Notes: ....

BEINN LIATH MHOR

Region	Area	Height
Applecross to Achnasheen	Highland	926 M / 3038 FEET

Date: .... Munro order: ....

Duration: .... Summit time: ....

Distance covered: .... Start time: ___:___   Finish time: ___:___

Companions: ....

─── Weather condition: ───

☀ ⛅ 🌥 🌧 ⛈ 🌨

─── Rating ───

Difficulty: ☆ ☆ ☆ ☆ ☆

Relish: ☆ ☆ ☆ ☆ ☆

Memories: ☆ ☆ ☆ ☆ ☆

PICTURE HERE

Notes: ....

GEAL CHARN

Region	Area	Height
Glen Albyn and the Monadh Liath	Highland	926 M / 3038 FEET

Date: ....

Munro order: ....

Duration: ....

Summit time: ....

Distance covered: ....

Start time: ___:___   Finish time: ___:___

Companions: ....
....

— Rating —
Difficulty: ☆☆☆☆☆
Relish: ☆☆☆☆☆
Memories: ☆☆☆☆☆

— Weather condition: —
☀ ⛅ ☁ 🌧 ⛈ 🌨

Notes: ....
....

SEANA BHRAIGH

Region	Area	Height
Loch Broom to Strath Oykel	Highland	926 M / 3038 FEET

Date: .... Munro order: ....

Duration: .... Summit time: ....

Distance covered: .... Start time: ___:___   Finish time: ___:___

Companions: ....

....

Weather condition:
☐ ☀ ☐ ⛅ ☐ 🌫 ☐ 🌧 ☐ ⛈ ☐ 🌨

Rating
Difficulty: ☆☆☆☆☆
Relish: ☆☆☆☆☆
Memories: ☆☆☆☆☆

PICTURE HERE

Notes: ....

....

SGURR NAN EAG

Region	Area	Height
Loch Arkaig to Glen Moriston	Highland	926.3 M / 3039 FEET

Date: .... Munro order: ....

Duration: .... Summit time: ....

Distance covered: .... Start time: ___:___   Finish time: ___:___

Companions: ....

....

───── Weather condition: ─────

☀️ ⛅ 🌥️ 🌧️ ⛈️ 🌨️

───── Rating ─────

Difficulty: ☆☆☆☆☆

Relish: ☆☆☆☆☆

Memories: ☆☆☆☆☆

Notes: ....

....

BEINN NARNAIN

Region	Area	Height
Inveraray to Crianlarich	Argyll and Bute	927 M /3041 FEET

Date: .... Munro order: ....

Duration: .... Summit time: ....

Distance covered: .... Start time: ___:___   Finish time: ___:___

Companions: ....

....

Weather condition: ☀ ⛅ ☁ 🌧 ⛈ 🌨

Rating
Difficulty: ☆☆☆☆☆
Relish: ☆☆☆☆☆
Memories: ☆☆☆☆☆

PICTURE HERE

Notes: ....

....

BEN HOPE

Region	Area	Height
Durness to Loch Shin	Highland	927 M / 3041 FEET

Date: .... Munro order: ....

Duration: .... Summit time: ....

Distance covered: .... Start time: ___:___   Finish time: ___:___

Companions: ....

....

— Weather condition: —   — Rating —

☐ ☀ ☐ ⛅ ☐ ☁ ☐ 🌧 ☐ ⛈ ☐ 🌨

Difficulty: ☆ ☆ ☆ ☆ ☆
Relish: ☆ ☆ ☆ ☆ ☆
Memories: ☆ ☆ ☆ ☆ ☆

Notes: ....

....

EIDIDH NAN CLACH GEALA

Region	Area	Height
Loch Broom to Strath Oykel	Highland	927 M / 3041 FEET

Date: ....

Munro order: ....

Duration: ....

Summit time: ....

Distance covered: ....

Start time: ___:___   Finish time: ___:___

Companions: ....
....
....

─── Rating ───
Difficulty: ☆ ☆ ☆ ☆ ☆
Relish: ☆ ☆ ☆ ☆ ☆
Memories: ☆ ☆ ☆ ☆ ☆

─── Weather condition: ───
☐ ☀ ☐ ⛅ ☐ ☁ ☐ 🌧 ☐ ⛈ ☐ 🌨

PICTURE HERE

Notes: ....
....

MAYAR

Region	Area	Height
Braemar to Montrose	Angus	928 M / 3045 FEET

Date: .... Munro order: ....

Duration: .... Summit time: ....

Distance covered: .... Start time: ___:___   Finish time: ___:___

Companions: ....

....

....

Weather condition:

☐ ☀ ☐ ⛅ ☐ ☁ ☐ 🌧 ☐ ⛈ ☐ 🌨

Rating

Difficulty: ☆☆☆☆☆

Relish: ☆☆☆☆☆

Memories: ☆☆☆☆☆

Notes: ....

....

MEALL NAN EUN

Region	Area	Height
Glen Etive to Glen Lochy	Argyll and Bute	928 M /3045 FEET

Date: .... Munro order: ....

Duration: .... Summit time: ....

Distance covered: .... Start time: ___:___   Finish time: ___:___

Companions: ....
....

Weather condition

☀ ⛅ 🌥 🌧 ⛈ 🌨

Rating

Difficulty: ☆ ☆ ☆ ☆ ☆
Relish: ☆ ☆ ☆ ☆ ☆
Memories: ☆ ☆ ☆ ☆ ☆

Notes: ....
....

MORUISG

Region	Area	Height
Kyle of Lochalsh to Garve	Highland	928 M /3045 FEET

Date: .... Munro order: ....

Duration: .... Summit time: ....

Distance covered: .... Start time: ___:___   Finish time: ___:___

Companions: ....

....

Rating
- Difficulty: ☆☆☆☆☆
- Relish: ☆☆☆☆☆
- Memories: ☆☆☆☆☆

Weather condition: ☀ ⛅ 🌥 🌧 ⛈ 🌨

PICTURE HERE

Notes: ....

....

BLA BHEINN

Region	Area	Height
Minginish and the Cuillin Hills	Highland	929 M / 3048 FEET

Date: ....

Munro order: ....

Duration: ....

Summit time: ....

Distance covered: ....

Start time: ___:___   Finish time: ___:___

Companions: ....
....
....

— Rating —
Difficulty: ☆ ☆ ☆ ☆ ☆
Relish: ☆ ☆ ☆ ☆ ☆
Memories: ☆ ☆ ☆ ☆ ☆

— Weather condition: —
☐ ☀ ☐ ⛅ ☐ ☁ ☐ 🌧 ☐ ⛈ ☐ 🌨

Notes: ....
....

A' CHAILLEACH

Region	Area	Height
Glen Albyn and the Monadh Liath	Highland	929.2 M /3049 FEET

Date: .... Munro order: ....

Duration: .... Summit time: ....

Distance covered: .... Start time: ___:___ Finish time: ___:___

Companions: ....
....

— Weather condition: —

— Rating —
Difficulty: ☆☆☆☆☆
Relish: ☆☆☆☆☆
Memories: ☆☆☆☆☆

Notes: ....
....

BEINN BHREAC

Region	Area	Height
Cairngorms	Aberdeenshire	931 M /3054 FEET

Date: .... Munro order: ....

Duration: .... Summit time: ....

Distance covered: .... Start time: ___:___   Finish time: ___:___

Companions: ....

──────── Weather condition: ──────── ──── Rating ────

☐ ☀ ☐ ⛅ ☐ ☁ ☐ 🌧 ☐ ⛈ ☐ 🌨

Difficulty: ☆☆☆☆☆
Relish: ☆☆☆☆☆
Memories: ☆☆☆☆☆

Notes: ....

BEN CHONZIE

Region	Area	Height
Glen Etive to Glen Lochy	Argyll and Bute	931 M / 3054 FEET

Date: .... Munro order: ....

Duration: .... Summit time: ....

Distance covered: .... Start time: ___:___   Finish time: ___:___

Companions: ....

....

Weather condition:
☐ ☀ ☐ ⛅ ☐ ☁ ☐ 🌧 ☐ ⛈ ☐ 🌨

Rating
Difficulty: ☆☆☆☆☆
Relish: ☆☆☆☆☆
Memories: ☆☆☆☆☆

Notes: ....
....

MEALL BUIDHE

Region	Area	Height
Loch Rannoch to Glen Lyon	Perth and Kinross	932.1 M / 3058 FEET

Date: ....

Munro order: ....

Duration: ....

Summit time: ....

Distance covered: ....

Start time: ___:___   Finish time: ___:___

Companions: ....
....
....

Rating
Difficulty: ☆☆☆☆☆
Relish: ☆☆☆☆☆
Memories: ☆☆☆☆☆

Weather condition:
☐ ☀ ☐ ⛅ ☐ ☁ ☐ 🌧 ☐ ⛈ ☐ 🌨

PICTURE HERE

Notes: ....
....

BEINN CHARBHAIR

Region	Area	Height
Loch Lomond to Strathyre	Stirling	932.2 M /3058 FEET

Date: .... Munro order: ....

Duration: .... Summit time: ....

Distance covered: .... Start time: ___:___   Finish time: ___:___

Companions: ....

....

Weather condition: ☀ ⛅ ☁ 🌧 ⛈ 🌨

Rating
Difficulty: ☆☆☆☆☆
Relish: ☆☆☆☆☆
Memories: ☆☆☆☆☆

Notes: ....

FIONN BHEINN

Region	Area	Height
The Fannaichs	Highland	933 M /3061 FEET

Date: ....

Duration: ....

Distance covered: ....

Companions: ....
....
....

Munro order: ....

Summit time: ....

Start time: ___:___   Finish time: ___:___

— Weather condition: —
☐ ☀ ☐ ⛅ ☐ ☁ ☐ 🌧 ☐ ⛈ ☐ 🌨

— Rating —
Difficulty: ☆ ☆ ☆ ☆ ☆
Relish: ☆ ☆ ☆ ☆ ☆
Memories: ☆ ☆ ☆ ☆ ☆

Notes: ....
....

MAOL CHEAN-DEARG

Region	Area	Height
Applecross to Achnasheen	Highland	933 M /3061 FEET

Date: .... Munro order: ....

Duration: .... Summit time: ....

Distance covered: .... Start time: ___:___   Finish time: ___:___

Companions: ....

Rating

Difficulty: ☆☆☆☆☆

Relish: ☆☆☆☆☆

Memories: ☆☆☆☆☆

Weather condition: ☀ ⛅ ☁ 🌧 ⛈ 🌨

Notes: ....

THE CAIRNWELL

Region	Area	Height
Loch Arkaig to Glen Moriston	Highland	933 M / 3061 FEET

Date: .... Munro order: ....

Duration: .... Summit time: ....

Distance covered: .... Start time: ___:___   Finish time: ___:___

Companions: ....
....

Weather condition:
☀️ ⛅ ☁️ 🌧️ ⛈️ 🌨️

Rating
Difficulty: ☆☆☆☆☆
Relish: ☆☆☆☆☆
Memories: ☆☆☆☆☆

PICTURE HERE

Notes: ....
....

BEINN TARSUINN

Region	Area	Height
Locj Maree to Loch Broom	Highland	933.8 M /3064 FEET

Date: .... Munro order: ....

Duration: .... Summit time: ....

Distance covered: .... Start time: ___:___   Finish time: ___:___

Companions: ....

....

— Weather condition: —   — Rating —

☀ ⛅ 🌫 🌧 ⛈ 🌨

Difficulty: ☆☆☆☆☆
Relish: ☆☆☆☆☆
Memories: ☆☆☆☆☆

Notes: ....

....

AM BASTEIR

Region	Area	Height
Minginish and the Cuillin Hills	Highland	934 M / 3064 FEET

Date: ....

Duration: ....

Distance covered: ....

Companions: ....
....
....

Munro order: ....

Summit time: ....

Start time: ___:___   Finish time: ___:___

──── Weather condition: ────
☐ ☀️ ☐ ⛅ ☐ 🌥️ ☐ 🌧️ ☐ ⛈️ ☐ 🌨️

──── Rating ────
Difficulty: ☆☆☆☆☆
Relish: ☆☆☆☆☆
Memories: ☆☆☆☆☆

PICTURE HERE

Notes: ....
....

41

MEALL A' CHRASGAIDH

Region	Area	Height
The Fannaichs	Highland	934 M / 3064 FEET

Date: .... Munro order: ....

Duration: .... Summit time: ....

Distance covered: .... Start time: ___:___   Finish time: ___:___

Companions: ....
....
....

— Weather condition: —
☀ ⛅ ☁ 🌧 ⛈ 🌨

— Rating —
Difficulty: ☆ ☆ ☆ ☆ ☆
Relish: ☆ ☆ ☆ ☆ ☆
Memories: ☆ ☆ ☆ ☆ ☆

PICTURE HERE

Notes: ....
....

42

BEINN NA LAP

Region	Area	Height
Loch Treig to Loch Ericht	Highland	935 M / 3068 FEET

Date: .... Munro order: ....

Duration: .... Summit time: ....

Distance covered: .... Start time: ___:___   Finish time: ___:___

Companions: ....
....

Weather condition:
☐ ☀ ☐ ⛅ ☐ ☁ ☐ 🌧 ☐ ⛈ ☐ 🌨

Rating
Difficulty: ☆☆☆☆☆
Relish: ☆☆☆☆☆
Memories: ☆☆☆☆☆

Notes: ....
....

A' BHUIDHEANACH BHEAG

Region	Area	Height
Loch Ericht to Glen Tromie & Glen	Highland /Perth and Kinross	936M /3071 FEET

Date: .... Munro order: ....

Duration: .... Summit time: ....

Distance covered: .... Start time: ___:___   Finish time: ___:___

Companions: ....

....

Weather condition: ☀ ⛅ ☁ 🌧 ⛈ 🌨

Rating
Difficulty: ☆☆☆☆☆
Relish: ☆☆☆☆☆
Memories: ☆☆☆☆☆

Notes: ....

....

BEINN SGULAIRD

Region	Area	Height
Loch Linnhe to Loch Etive	Argyll and Bute	937 M /3074 FEET

Date: ....

Munro order: ....

Duration: ....

Summit time: ....

Distance covered: ....

Start time: ___:___   Finish time: ___:___

Companions: ....
....
....

Rating
Difficulty: ☆☆☆☆☆
Relish: ☆☆☆☆☆
Memories: ☆☆☆☆☆

Weather condition:
☀ ⛅ ☁ 🌧 ⛈ 🌨

PICTURE HERE

Notes: ....
....

SRON A' CHOIRE GHAIRBH

Region	Area	Height
Loch Rannoch to Glen Lyon	Perth and Kinross	937 M / 3074 FEET

Date: .... Munro order: ....

Duration: .... Summit time: ....

Distance covered: .... Start time: ___:___   Finish time: ___:___

Companions: ....
....

Weather condition:
☀ ☁ 🌫 🌧 ⛈ 🌨

Rating
Difficulty: ☆☆☆☆☆
Relish: ☆☆☆☆☆
Memories: ☆☆☆☆☆

Notes: ....
....

LUINNE BHEINN

Region	Area	Height
Knoydart to Glen Kingie	Highland	939 M / 3081 FEET

Date: .... Munro order: ....

Duration: .... Summit time: ....

Distance covered: .... Start time: ___:___   Finish time: ___:___

Companions: ....
....
....

— Weather condition: —

— Rating —

Difficulty: ☆☆☆☆☆
Relish: ☆☆☆☆☆
Memories: ☆☆☆☆☆

Notes: ....
....

MOUNT KEEN

Region	Area	Height
Braemar to Montrose	Aberdeenshire/Angus	939 M /3081 FEET

Date: .... Munro order: ....

Duration: .... Summit time: ....

Distance covered: .... Start time: ___:___   Finish time: ___:___

Companions: ....

— Weather condition: —

☐ ☀ ☐ ⛅ ☐ 🌥 ☐ 🌧 ☐ ⛈ ☐ 🌨

— Rating —

Difficulty: ☆ ☆ ☆ ☆ ☆

Relish: ☆ ☆ ☆ ☆ ☆

Memories: ☆ ☆ ☆ ☆ ☆

PICTURE HERE

Notes: ....

MULLACH NAN COIREAN

Region	Area	Height
Fort William to Loch Treig & Loch Leven	Highland	939.3 M / 3082 FEET

Date: ....

Munro order: ....

Duration: ....

Summit time: ....

Distance covered: ....

Start time: ___:___   Finish time: ___:___

Companions: ....
....

― Rating ―
Difficulty: ☆ ☆ ☆ ☆ ☆
Relish: ☆ ☆ ☆ ☆ ☆
Memories: ☆ ☆ ☆ ☆ ☆

― Weather condition: ―
☀ ⛅ ☁ 🌧 ⛈ 🌨

Notes: ....
....

CARN NA CAIM

Region	Area	Height
Loch Ericht to Glen Tromie & Glen Garry	Highland /Perth and Kinross	940.8 M /3087 FEET

Date: .... Munro order: ....

Duration: .... Summit time: ....

Distance covered: .... Start time: ___:___   Finish time: ___:___

Companions: ....
....

Weather condition:

☐ ☀ ☐ ⛅ ☐ ☁ ☐ 🌧 ☐ ⛈ ☐ 🌨

Rating

Difficulty: ☆☆☆☆☆
Relish: ☆☆☆☆☆
Memories: ☆☆☆☆☆

Notes: ....
....

CARN DEARG

Region	Area	Height
Loch Treig to Loch Ericht	Highland /Perth and Kinross	941 M /3087 FEET

Date: .... Munro order: ....

Duration: .... Summit time: ....

Distance covered: .... Start time: ___:___   Finish time: ___:___

Companions: ....

....

--- Weather condition: ---   Rating

Difficulty: ☆☆☆☆☆

Relish: ☆☆☆☆☆

Memories: ☆☆☆☆☆

☀ ⛅ 🌥 🌧 ⛈ 🌨

Notes: ....
....

BEINN A' CHROIN

Region	Area	Height
Loch Lomond to Strathyre	Stirling	941.4 M /3089 FEET

Date: .... Munro order: ....

Duration: .... Summit time: ....

Distance covered: .... Start time: ___:___   Finish time: ___:___

Companions: ....

....

Weather condition: ☀ ⛅ ☁ 🌧 ⛈ 🌨

Rating

Difficulty: ☆☆☆☆☆

Relish: ☆☆☆☆☆

Memories: ☆☆☆☆☆

Notes: ....

BEN VORLICH

Region	Area	Height
Inveraray to Crianlarich	Agryll and Bute	943 M /3094FEET

Date: .... Munro order: ....

Duration: .... Summit time: ....

Distance covered: .... Start time: ___:___   Finish time: ___:___

Companions: ....

....

Weather condition:

☐ ☀ ☐ ⛅ ☐ ☁ ☐ 🌧 ☐ ⛈ ☐ 🌨

Rating

Difficulty: ☆ ☆ ☆ ☆ ☆

Relish: ☆ ☆ ☆ ☆ ☆

Memories: ☆ ☆ ☆ ☆ ☆

Notes: ....

....

BINNEIN BEAG

Region	Area	Height
Fort William to Loch Treig & Loch Leven	Highland	943 M / 3094 FEET

Date: .... Munro order: ....

Duration: .... Summit time: ....

Distance covered: .... Start time: ___:___   Finish time: ___:___

Companions: ....

....

Weather condition: ☀ ⛅ 🌫 🌧 ⛈ 🌨

Rating
- Difficulty: ☆☆☆☆☆
- Relish: ☆☆☆☆☆
- Memories: ☆☆☆☆☆

Notes: ....

....

AN SOCACH

Region	Area	Height
Pitlochry to Braemar & Blairgowrie	Aberdeenshire	944 M / 3097 FEET

Date: .... Munro order: ....

Duration: .... Summit time: ....

Distance covered: .... Start time: ___:___   Finish time: ___:___

Companions: ....
....

Weather condition:
☐ ☀ ☐ ⛅ ☐ ☁ ☐ 🌧 ☐ ⛈ ☐ 🌨

Rating
Difficulty: ☆☆☆☆☆
Relish: ☆☆☆☆☆
Memories: ☆☆☆☆☆

Notes: ....
....

SGURR DUBH MOR

Region	Area	Height
Loch Rannoch to Glen Lyon	Perth and Kinross	944 M / 3097 FEET

Date: .... Munro order: ....

Duration: .... Summit time: ....

Distance covered: .... Start time: ___:___   Finish time: ___:___

Companions: ....

....

— Weather condition: —

☀ ⛅ ☁ 🌧 ⛈ 🌨

— Rating —

Difficulty: ☆☆☆☆☆

Relish: ☆☆☆☆☆

Memories: ☆☆☆☆☆

PICTURE HERE

Notes: ....

....

BIDEAN A' CHOIRE SHEASGAICH

Region	Area	Height
Kyle of Lochalsh to Garve	Highland	945 M /3100 FEET

Date: .... Munro order: ....

Duration: .... Summit time: ....

Distance covered: .... Start time: ___:___   Finish time: ___:___

Companions: ....

....

Weather condition: ☐ ☀ ☐ ⛅ ☐ 🌥 ☐ 🌧 ☐ ⛈ ☐ 🌨

Rating
Difficulty: ☆☆☆☆☆
Relish: ☆☆☆☆☆
Memories: ☆☆☆☆☆

PICTURE HERE

Notes: ....
....

STOB A' CHOIRE ODHAIR

Region	Area	Height
Loch Rannoch to Glen Lyon	Perth and Kinross	945 M /3100 FEET

Date: .... Munro order: ....

Duration: .... Summit time: ....

Distance covered: .... Start time: ___:___   Finish time: ___:___

Companions: ....

....

....

Weather condition: ☀ ☁ 🌥 🌧 ⛈ 🌨

Rating
- Difficulty: ☆☆☆☆☆
- Relish: ☆☆☆☆☆
- Memories: ☆☆☆☆☆

Notes: ....

....

CARN BHAC

Region	Area	Height
Pitlochry to Braemar & Blairgowrie	Aberdeenshire	945.1 M / 3101 FEET

Date: .... Munro order: ....

Duration: .... Summit time: ....

Distance covered: .... Start time: ___:___   Finish time: ___:___

Companions: ....
....

Weather condition:
☐ ☀ ☐ ⛅ ☐ ☁ ☐ 🌧 ☐ ⛈ ☐ 🌨

Rating
Difficulty: ☆☆☆☆☆
Relish: ☆☆☆☆☆
Memories: ☆☆☆☆☆

PICTURE HERE

Notes: ....
....

CARN DEARG

Region	Area	Height
Glen Albyn and the Monadh Liath	Highland	945.7 M /3103 FEET

Date: .... Munro order: ....

Duration: .... Summit time: ....

Distance covered: .... Start time: ___:___   Finish time: ___:___

Companions: ....

....

Weather condition: ☀ ⛅ ☁ 🌧 ⛈ 🌨

Rating
Difficulty: ☆☆☆☆☆
Relish: ☆☆☆☆☆
Memories: ☆☆☆☆☆

Notes: ....

....

BEINN TULAICHEAN

Region	Area	Height
Loch Lomond to Strathyre	Stirling	945.8 M / 3103 FEET

Date: .... Munro order: ....

Duration: .... Summit time: ....

Distance covered: .... Start time: ___:___   Finish time: ___:___

Companions: ....
....

Rating
Difficulty: ☆☆☆☆☆
Relish: ☆☆☆☆☆
Memories: ☆☆☆☆☆

Weather condition:
☀ ⛅ ☁ 🌧 ⛈ 🌨

PICTURE HERE

Notes: ....
....

CREAG A' MHAIM

Region	Area	Height
Glen Shiel to Loch Hourn and Loch Quoich	Highland	946 M / 3104 FEET

Date: .... Munro order: ....

Duration: .... Summit time: ....

Distance covered: .... Start time: ___:___   Finish time: ___:___

Companions: ....

....

Weather condition: ☀ ⛅ ☁ 🌧 ⛈ 🌨

Rating
Difficulty: ☆☆☆☆☆
Relish: ☆☆☆☆☆
Memories: ☆☆☆☆☆

Notes: ....

....

SGURR NA SGINE

Region	Area	Height
Loch Rannoch to Glen Lyon	Perth and Kinross	946 M / 3104 FEET

Date: ....

Munro order: ....

Duration: ....

Summit time: ....

Distance covered: ....

Start time: ___:___   Finish time: ___:___

Companions: ....
....

Rating
Difficulty: ☆☆☆☆☆
Relish: ☆☆☆☆☆
Memories: ☆☆☆☆☆

Weather condition:
☐ ☀ ☐ ⛅ ☐ ☁ ☐ 🌧 ☐ ⛈ ☐ 🌨

PICTURE HERE

Notes: ....
....

MEALL BUIDHE

Region	Area	Height
Knoydart to Glen Kingie	Highland	946 M / 3104 FEET

Date: ……………………………………………   Munro order: ……………………………………………

Duration: ………………………………………   Summit time: ……………………………………………

Distance covered: ……………………………   Start time: ___:___   Finish time: ___:___

Companions: ……………………………………………………………………
………………………………………………………………………………………

Weather condition: ☀ ⛅ ☁ 🌧 ⛈ 🌨

Rating
- Difficulty: ☆☆☆☆☆
- Relish: ☆☆☆☆☆
- Memories: ☆☆☆☆☆

Notes: ……
……

DRIESH

Region	Area	Height
Braemar to Montrose	Angus	947 M / 3107 FEET

Date: .... Munro order: ....

Duration: .... Summit time: ....

Distance covered: .... Start time: ___:___   Finish time: ___:___

Companions: ....

....

Weather condition: ☀ ⛅ ☁ 🌧 ⛈ 🌨

Rating
- Difficulty: ☆☆☆☆☆
- Relish: ☆☆☆☆☆
- Memories: ☆☆☆☆☆

Notes: ....

....

SGURR MHIC CHOINNICH

Region	Area	Height
Loch Rannoch to Glen Lyon	Perth and Kinross	948.1 M /3110 FEET

Date: ....

Munro order: ....

Duration: ....

Summit time: ....

Distance covered: ....

Start time: ___:___   Finish time: ___:___

Companions: ....
....

Rating
Difficulty: ☆☆☆☆☆
Relish: ☆☆☆☆☆
Memories: ☆☆☆☆☆

Weather condition: ☐ ☐ ☐ ☐ ☐ ☐

Notes: ....
....

BEINN BHUIDHE

Region	Area	Height
Inveraray to Crinlarich	Argyll and Bute	948.5 M /3112 FEET

Date: .... Munro order: ....

Duration: .... Summit time: ....

Distance covered: .... Start time: ___:___   Finish time: ___:___

Companions: ....
....

— Weather condition: —
☀ ⛅ 🌥 🌧 ⛈ 🌨

— Rating —
Difficulty: ☆☆☆☆☆
Relish: ☆☆☆☆☆
Memories: ☆☆☆☆☆

PICTURE HERE

Notes: ....
....

MEALL GORM

Region	Area	Height
The Fannaichs	Highland	949 M / 3114 FEET

Date: .... Munro order: ....

Duration: .... Summit time: ....

Distance covered: .... Start time: ___:___   Finish time: ___:___

Companions: ....

....

Weather condition:
☀ ⛅ ☁ 🌧 ⛈ 🌨

Rating
Difficulty: ☆☆☆☆☆
Relish: ☆☆☆☆☆
Memories: ☆☆☆☆☆

Notes: ....

....

MEALL CHUAICH

Region	Area	Height
Loch Ericht to Glen Tromie & Glen Garry	Highland	951 M / 3120 FEET

Date: .... Munro order: ....

Duration: .... Summit time: ....

Distance covered: .... Start time: ___:___   Finish time: ___:___

Companions: ....
....
....

Weather condition:
☀ ⛅ 🌥 🌧 ⛈ 🌨

Rating
Difficulty: ☆☆☆☆☆
Relish: ☆☆☆☆☆
Memories: ☆☆☆☆☆

Notes: ....
....

AONACH EAGACH
MEALL DEARG

Region	Area	Height
Loch Leven to Rannoch Station	Highland	952.3 M /3124 FEET

Date: .... Munro order: ....

Duration: .... Summit time: ....

Distance covered: .... Start time: ___:___   Finish time: ___:___

Companions: ....
....

— Weather condition: —   — Rating —

☀ ⛅ 🌫 🌧 ⛈ 🌨

Difficulty: ☆☆☆☆☆
Relish: ☆☆☆☆☆
Memories: ☆☆☆☆☆

Notes: ....
....

BEINN MHANACH

Region	Area	Height
Loch Rannoch to Glen Lyon	Perth and Kinross	953 M /3127 FEET

Date: .... Munro order: ....

Duration: .... Summit time: ....

Distance covered: .... Start time: ___:___   Finish time: ___:___

Companions: ....
....

— Weather condition: —

☀ ⛅ ☁ 🌧 ⛈ 🌨

— Rating —
Difficulty: ☆ ☆ ☆ ☆ ☆
Relish: ☆ ☆ ☆ ☆ ☆
Memories: ☆ ☆ ☆ ☆ ☆

Notes: ....
....

AM FAOCHAGACH

Region	Area	Height
Loch Broom to Strath Oykel	Highland	953 M /3127 FEET

Date: .... Munro order: ....

Duration: .... Summit time: ....

Distance covered: .... Start time: ___:___   Finish time: ___:___

Companions: ....

....

Weather condition: ☀ ⛅ ☁ 🌧 ⛈ 🌨

Rating
Difficulty: ☆☆☆☆☆
Relish: ☆☆☆☆☆
Memories: ☆☆☆☆☆

Notes: ....
....

BUACHAILLE ETIVE MOR
STOB NA BROIGE

Region	Area	Height
Loch Linnhe to Loch Etive	Highland	953.4 M / 3128 FEET

Date: ....

Munro order: ....

Duration: ....

Summit time: ....

Distance covered: ....

Start time: ___:___   Finish time: ___:___

Companions: ....
....

— Weather condition: —
☀ ⛅ ☁ 🌧 ⛈ 🌨

— Rating —
Difficulty: ☆☆☆☆☆
Relish: ☆☆☆☆☆
Memories: ☆☆☆☆☆

PICTURE HERE

Notes: ....
....

SGURR NAN COIREACHAN

Region	Area	Height
Loch Rannoch to Glen Lyon	Perth and Kinross	953.8 M /3129 FEET

Date: .... Munro order: ....

Duration: .... Summit time: ....

Distance covered: .... Start time: ___:___   Finish time: ___:___

Companions: ....

....

Rating

Difficulty: ☆ ☆ ☆ ☆ ☆

Relish: ☆ ☆ ☆ ☆ ☆

Memories: ☆ ☆ ☆ ☆ ☆

Weather condition: ☀ ⛅ ☁ 🌧 ⛈ 🌨

Notes: ....

....

BEINN LIATH MHOR FANNAICH

Region	Area	Height
The Fannaichs	Highland	954 M /3130 FEET

Date: .... Munro order: ....

Duration: .... Summit time: ....

Distance covered: .... Start time: ___:___   Finish time: ___:___

Companions: ....
....

Weather condition:
☐ ☀ ☐ ⛅ ☐ ☁ ☐ 🌧 ☐ ⛈ ☐ 🌨

Rating
Difficulty: ☆☆☆☆☆
Relish: ☆☆☆☆☆
Memories: ☆☆☆☆☆

PICTURE HERE

Notes: ....
....

SGOR GAIBHRE

Region	Area	Height
Loch Treig to Loch Ericht	Highland/ Perth and Kinross	955 M /3133 FEET

Date: .... Munro order: ....

Duration: .... Summit time: ....

Distance covered: .... Start time: ___:___   Finish time: ___:___

Companions: ....

....

Weather condition: ☐ ☀ ☐ ⛅ ☐ 🌥 ☐ 🌧 ☐ ⛈ ☐ 🌨

Rating
Difficulty: ☆☆☆☆☆
Relish: ☆☆☆☆☆
Memories: ☆☆☆☆☆

Notes: ....

....

SGURR NAN CONBHAIREAN

Region	Area	Height
Loch Arkaig to Glen Moriston	Highland	1109 M / 3638 FEET

Date: ....

Munro order: ....

Duration: ....

Summit time: ....

Distance covered: ....

Start time: ___:___   Finish time: ___:___

Companions: ....
....
....

Rating

Difficulty: ☆☆☆☆☆
Relish: ☆☆☆☆☆
Memories: ☆☆☆☆☆

Weather condition:
☐ ☀ ☐ ⛅ ☐ ☁ ☐ 🌧 ☐ ⛈ ☐ 🌨

PICTURE HERE

Notes: ....
....

SAILEAG

Region	Area	Height
Loch Duich to Cannich	Highland	956 M / 3136 FEET

Date: .... Munro order: ....

Duration: .... Summit time: ....

Distance covered: .... Start time: ___:___   Finish time: ___:___

Companions: ....

....

— Weather condition: —

☀ 🌤 🌫 🌧 ⛈ 🌨

— Rating —

Difficulty: ☆☆☆☆☆

Relish: ☆☆☆☆☆

Memories: ☆☆☆☆☆

Notes: ....
....

TOM BUIDHE

Region	Area	Height
Loch Arkaig to Glen Moriston	Highland	957 M / 3140 FEET

Date: ....

Duration: ....

Distance covered: ....

Companions: ....
....
....

Munro order: ....

Summit time: ....

Start time: ___:___   Finish time: ___:___

— Rating —
Difficulty: ☆☆☆☆☆
Relish: ☆☆☆☆☆
Memories: ☆☆☆☆☆

— Weather condition: —
☀ ⛅ ☁ 🌧 ⛈ 🌨

PICTURE HERE

Notes: ....
....

CARN GHLUASAID

Region	Area	Height
Glen Affric to Glen Moriston	Highland	957 M / 3140 FEET

Date: .... Munro order: ....

Duration: .... Summit time: ....

Distance covered: .... Start time: ___:___   Finish time: ___:___

Companions: ....
....

Rating
Difficulty: ☆☆☆☆☆
Relish: ☆☆☆☆☆
Memories: ☆☆☆☆☆

Weather condition:
☀ ⛅ ☁ 🌧 ⛈ 🌨

Notes: ....
....

BUACHAILLE ETIVE BEAG
STOP DUBH

Region	Area	Height
Loch Linnhe to Loch Etive	Highland	958 M / 3143 FEET

Date: .... Munro order: ....

Duration: .... Summit time: ....

Distance covered: .... Start time: ___:___   Finish time: ___:___

Companions: ....

─ Rating ─

Difficulty: ☆ ☆ ☆ ☆ ☆

Relish: ☆ ☆ ☆ ☆ ☆

Memories: ☆ ☆ ☆ ☆ ☆

─ Weather condition: ─

☐ ☀ ☐ ⛅ ☐ ☁ ☐ 🌧 ☐ ⛈ ☐ 🌨

PICTURE HERE

Notes: ....
....

TOLMOUNT

Region	Area	Height
Loch Arkaig to Glen Moriston	Highland	958 M /3143 FEET

Date: .... Munro order: ....

Duration: .... Summit time: ....

Distance covered: .... Start time: ___:___   Finish time: ___:___

Companions: ....

....

....

— Weather condition: —

☀ ⛅ ☁ 🌧 ⛈ 🌨

— Rating —

Difficulty: ☆ ☆ ☆ ☆ ☆

Relish: ☆ ☆ ☆ ☆ ☆

Memories: ☆ ☆ ☆ ☆ ☆

Notes: ....

....

BRUACH NA FRITHE

Region	Area	Height
Minginish and the Cuillin Hills	Highland	958.8 M /3143 FEET

Date: .... Munro order: ....

Duration: .... Summit time: ....

Distance covered: .... Start time: ___:___   Finish time: ___:___

Companions: ....

....

Weather condition:

☐ ☀ ☐ ⛅ ☐ ☁ ☐ 🌧 ☐ ⛈ ☐ 🌨

Rating

Difficulty: ☆ ☆ ☆ ☆ ☆

Relish: ☆ ☆ ☆ ☆ ☆

Memories: ☆ ☆ ☆ ☆ ☆

PICTURE HERE

Notes: ....

....

MEALL GLAS

Region	Area	Height
glen Lyon to Glen Dochart & Loch Tay	Stirling	959 M / 3146 FEET

Date: .... Munro order: ....

Duration: .... Summit time: ....

Distance covered: .... Start time: ___:___   Finish time: ___:___

Companions: ....
....

Weather condition:
☐ ☀ ☐ ⛅ ☐ ☁ ☐ 🌧 ☐ ⛈ ☐ 🌨

Rating
Difficulty: ☆ ☆ ☆ ☆ ☆
Relish: ☆ ☆ ☆ ☆ ☆
Memories: ☆ ☆ ☆ ☆ ☆

Notes: ....
....

BEINN FHIONNLAIDH

Region	Area	Height
Loch Duich to Cannich	Highland	1004.7 M / 3296 FEET

Date: ....

Munro order: ....

Duration: ....

Summit time: ....

Distance covered: ....

Start time: ___:___   Finish time: ___:___

Companions: ....
....

— Rating —
Difficulty: ☆ ☆ ☆ ☆ ☆
Relish: ☆ ☆ ☆ ☆ ☆
Memories: ☆ ☆ ☆ ☆ ☆

— Weather condition: —
☐ ☐ ☐ ☐ ☐ ☐
☀ ⛅ ☁ 🌧 ⛈ 🌨

PICTURE HERE

Notes: ....
....

BEINN NAN AIGHENAN

Region	Area	Height
Glen Etive to Glen Lochy	Argyll and Bute	960 M / 3150 FEET

Date: ....

Duration: ....

Distance covered: ....

Companions: ....
....
....

Munro order: ....

Summit time: ....

Start time: ___:___   Finish time: ___:___

Weather condition:
☐ ☀ ☐ ⛅ ☐ ☁ ☐ 🌧 ☐ ⛈ ☐ 🌨

Rating
Difficulty: ☆☆☆☆☆
Relish: ☆☆☆☆☆
Memories: ☆☆☆☆☆

PICTURE HERE

Notes: ....
....

STUCHD AN LOCHAIN

Region	Area	Height
The Fannaichs	Highland	960 M /3150 FEET

Date: .... Munro order: ....

Duration: .... Summit time: ....

Distance covered: .... Start time: ___:___   Finish time: ___:___

Companions: ....
....

— Weather condition: —

☀ ⛅ ☁ 🌧 ⛈ 🌨

— Rating —

Difficulty: ☆ ☆ ☆ ☆ ☆
Relish: ☆ ☆ ☆ ☆ ☆
Memories: ☆ ☆ ☆ ☆ ☆

Notes: ....
....

SGORR RUADH

Region	Area	Height
Applecross to Achnasheen	Highland	960.7 M /3152 FEET

Date: .... Munro order: ....

Duration: .... Summit time: ....

Distance covered: .... Start time: ___:___   Finish time: ___:___

Companions: ....

Weather condition: ☐ ☀ ☐ ⛅ ☐ ☁ ☐ 🌧 ☐ ⛈ ☐ 🌨

Rating
Difficulty: ☆☆☆☆☆
Relish: ☆☆☆☆☆
Memories: ☆☆☆☆☆

Notes: ....
....

BEN KLIBRECK

Region	Area	Height
Altnaharra to Dornoch	Highland	962.1 M /3156 FEET

Date: .... Munro order: ....

Duration: .... Summit time: ....

Distance covered: .... Start time: ___:___   Finish time: ___:___

Companions: ....

....

Weather condition: ☀ ⛅ ☁ 🌧 ⛈ 🌨

Rating
- Difficulty: ☆☆☆☆☆
- Relish: ☆☆☆☆☆
- Memories: ☆☆☆☆☆

Notes: ....

SGURR THUILM

Region	Area	Height
Loch Arkaig to Glen Moriston	Highland	963 M /3159 FEET

Date: ....

Duration: ....

Distance covered: ....

Companions: ....
....
....

Munro order: ....

Summit time: ....

Start time: ___:___   Finish time: ___:___

— Weather condition: —

— Rating —

Difficulty: ☆☆☆☆☆

Relish: ☆☆☆☆☆

Memories: ☆☆☆☆☆

Notes: ....
....

CAIRN A' CHLAMAIN

Region	Area	Height
Glen Tromie to Glen Tilt	Perth and Kinross	963.5 M / 3161 FEET

Date: .... Munro order: ....

Duration: .... Summit time: ....

Distance covered: .... Start time: ___:___   Finish time: ___:___

Companions: ....
....

Rating
Difficulty: ☆ ☆ ☆ ☆ ☆
Relish: ☆ ☆ ☆ ☆ ☆
Memories: ☆ ☆ ☆ ☆ ☆

Weather condition:
☐ ☀ ☐ ⛅ ☐ ☁ ☐ 🌧 ☐ ⛈ ☐ 🌨

PICTURE HERE

Notes: ....
....

SGURR NA BANACHDICH

Region	Area	Height
Loch Arkaig to Glen Moriston	Highland	965 M / 3166 FEET

Date: ....

Duration: ....

Distance covered: ....

Companions: ....
....
....

Munro order: ....

Summit time: ....

Start time: ___:___   Finish time: ___:___

Rating

Difficulty: ☆☆☆☆☆
Relish: ☆☆☆☆☆
Memories: ☆☆☆☆☆

Weather condition:
☐ ☀ ☐ ⛅ ☐ ☁ ☐ 🌧 ☐ ⛈ ☐ 🌨

Notes: ....
....

BEN MORE

Region	Area	Height
Mull and Nearby Islands	Argyll and Bute	966 M /3169 FEET

Date: .... Munro order: ....

Duration: .... Summit time: ....

Distance covered: .... Start time: ___:___   Finish time: ___:___

Companions: ....

....

....

— Weather condition: —

☐ ☀   ☐ ⛅   ☐ ☁   ☐ 🌧   ☐ ⛈   ☐ 🌨

— Rating —

Difficulty: ☆☆☆☆☆

Relish: ☆☆☆☆☆

Memories: ☆☆☆☆☆

Notes: ....

....

SGURR NAN GILLEAN

Region	Area	Height
Loch Rannoch to Glen Lyon	Perth and Kinross	966.1 M / 3170 FEET

Date: .... Munro order: ....

Duration: .... Summit time: ....

Distance covered: .... Start time: ___:___   Finish time: ___:___

Companions: ....

....

Weather condition:
☀️ ⛅ ☁️ 🌧️ ⛈️ 🌨️

Rating
Difficulty: ☆☆☆☆☆
Relish: ☆☆☆☆☆
Memories: ☆☆☆☆☆

Notes: ....
....

A' MHAIGHDEAN

Region	Area	Height
Loch Maree to Loch Broom	Highland	967 M / 3173 FEET

Date: .... Munro order: ....

Duration: .... Summit time: ....

Distance covered: .... Start time: ___:___   Finish time: ___:___

Companions: ....
....

—— Weather condition: ——

☀ ⛅ ☁ 🌧 ⛈ 🌨

—— Rating ——

Difficulty: ☆☆☆☆☆
Relish: ☆☆☆☆☆
Memories: ☆☆☆☆☆

PICTURE HERE

Notes: ....
....

AONACH EAGACH
SGORR NAM FIANNAIDH

Region	Area	Height
Loch Leven to Rannoch Station	Highland	967.7 M /3175 FEET

Date: .... Munro order: ....

Duration: .... Summit time: ....

Distance covered: .... Start time: ___:___   Finish time: ___:___

Companions: ....

....

Weather condition:

Rating

Difficulty: ☆☆☆☆☆

Relish: ☆☆☆☆☆

Memories: ☆☆☆☆☆

Notes: ....

....

MEALL GARBH

Region	Area	Height
Loch Rannoch to Glen Lyon	Perth and Kinross	968 M / 3176 FEET

Date: .... Munro order: ....

Duration: .... Summit time: ....

Distance covered: .... Start time: ___:___   Finish time: ___:___

Companions: ....

....

Weather condition: ☀ ⛅ 🌥 🌧 ⛈ 🌨

Rating
Difficulty: ☆☆☆☆☆
Relish: ☆☆☆☆☆
Memories: ☆☆☆☆☆

Notes: ....
....

SGURR A' GHREADAIDH

Region	Area	Height
Minginish and the Cuillin Hills	Highland	972.1 M / 3189 FEET

Date: ....

Munro order: ....

Duration: ....

Summit time: ....

Distance covered: ....

Start time: ___:___   Finish time: ___:___

Companions: ....
....
....

— Rating —

Difficulty: ☆☆☆☆☆

Relish: ☆☆☆☆☆

Memories: ☆☆☆☆☆

— Weather condition: —

☐ ☀ ☐ ⛅ ☐ ☁ ☐ 🌧 ☐ ⛈ ☐ 🌨

Notes: ....
....

A' MHARCONAICH

Region	Area	Height
Loch Ericht to Glen Tromie & Glen Garry	Highland	973.2 M / 3193 FEET

Date: .... Munro order: ....

Duration: .... Summit time: ....

Distance covered: .... Start time: ___:___   Finish time: ___:___

Companions: ....

....

....

— Weather condition: —

☀ ⛅ 🌥 🌧 ⛈ 🌨

— Rating —

Difficulty: ☆☆☆☆☆

Relish: ☆☆☆☆☆

Memories: ☆☆☆☆☆

PICTURE HERE

Notes: ....

....

BEN LOMOND

Region	Area	Height
Loch Lomond to Strathyre	Stirling	974 M / 3196 FEET

Date: .... Munro order: ....

Duration: .... Summit time: ....

Distance covered: .... Start time: ___:___   Finish time: ___:___

Companions: ....

— Rating —

Difficulty: ☆ ☆ ☆ ☆ ☆

Relish: ☆ ☆ ☆ ☆ ☆

Memories: ☆ ☆ ☆ ☆ ☆

— Weather condition: —

☐ ☀ ☐ ⛅ ☐ ☁ ☐ 🌧 ☐ ⛈ ☐ 🌨

Notes: ....
....

BEINN SGRITHEALL

Region	Area	Height
Glen Shiel to Loch Hourn and Loch Quoich	Highland	974 M /3,196 FEET

Date: .... Munro order: ....

Duration: .... Summit time: ....

Distance covered: .... Start time: ___:___   Finish time: ___:___

Companions: ....
....

— Weather condition: —
☀ ⛅ ☁ 🌧 ⛈ 🌨

— Rating —
Difficulty: ☆☆☆☆☆
Relish: ☆☆☆☆☆
Memories: ☆☆☆☆☆

PICTURE HERE

Notes: ....
....

STUC A' CHROIN

Region	Area	Height
Loch Arkaig to Glen Moriston	Highland	975 M / 3199 FEET

Date: .... Munro order: ....

Duration: .... Summit time: ....

Distance covered: .... Start time: ___:___   Finish time: ___:___

Companions: ....
....

— Weather condition: —

☀ ⛅ ☁ 🌧 ⛈ 🌨

— Rating —

Difficulty: ☆☆☆☆☆
Relish: ☆☆☆☆☆
Memories: ☆☆☆☆☆

Notes: ....
....

CAIRN A' GHEOIDH

Region	Area	Height
Pitlochry to Braemar & Blairgowrie	Aberdeenshire /Perth and Kinross	975 M /3199 FEET

Date: ....

Munro order: ....

Duration: ....

Summit time: ....

Distance covered: ....

Start time: ___:___   Finish time: ___:___

Companions: ....
....

Rating

Difficulty: ☆☆☆☆☆
Relish: ☆☆☆☆☆
Memories: ☆☆☆☆☆

Weather condition:
☀ ⛅ ☁ 🌧 ⛈ 🌨

PICTURE HERE

Notes: ....
....

BEINN A' GHLO
CARN LIATH

Region	Area	Height
Pitlochry to Braemar & Blairgowrie	Perth and Kinross	923.9 M /3704 FEET

Date: ....

Munro order: ....

Duration: ....

Summit time: ....

Distance covered: ....

Start time: ___:___   Finish time: ___:___

Companions: ....
....
....

Rating
Difficulty: ☆☆☆☆☆
Relish: ☆☆☆☆☆
Memories: ☆☆☆☆☆

Weather condition: ☀ ⛅ ☁ 🌧 ⛈ 🌨

Notes: ....
....

STOB BAN

Region	Area	Height
Loch Rannoch to Glen Lyon	Perth and Kinross	977 M /3205 FEET

Date: .... Munro order: ....

Duration: .... Summit time: ....

Distance covered: .... Start time: ___:___   Finish time: ___:___

Companions: ....

....

Weather condition: ☀ ⛅ ☁ 🌧 ⛈ 🌨

Rating
Difficulty: ☆☆☆☆☆
Relish: ☆☆☆☆☆
Memories: ☆☆☆☆☆

PICTURE HERE

Notes: ....
....

MEALL NAN CEAPRAICHEAN

Region	Area	Height
Loch Broom to Strath Oykel	Highland	977 M /3205 FEET

Date: ....

Munro order: ....

Duration: ....

Summit time: ....

Distance covered: ....

Start time: ___:___   Finish time: ___:___

Companions: ....
....
....

Rating
- Difficulty: ☆☆☆☆☆
- Relish: ☆☆☆☆☆
- Memories: ☆☆☆☆☆

Weather condition: ☀ ⛅ ☁ 🌧 ⛈ 🌨

Notes: ....
....

BEINN DUBHCHRAIG

Region	Area	Height
Loch Treig to Loch Ericht	Highland	978 M / 3209 FEET

Date: ....

Munro order: ....

Duration: ....

Summit time: ....

Distance covered: ....

Start time: ___:___   Finish time: ___:___

Companions: ....
....
....

Rating

Difficulty: ☆ ☆ ☆ ☆ ☆

Relish: ☆ ☆ ☆ ☆ ☆

Memories: ☆ ☆ ☆ ☆ ☆

Weather condition:
☐ ☀ ☐ ⛅ ☐ ☁ ☐ 🌧 ☐ ⛈ ☐ 🌨

PICTURE HERE

Notes: ....
....

CONA' MHEALL

Region	Area	Height
Loch Broom to Strath Oykel	Highland	978 M / 3209 FEET

Date: .... Munro order: ....

Duration: .... Summit time: ....

Distance covered: .... Start time: ___:___   Finish time: ___:___

Companions: ....

....

— Weather condition: —

— Rating —

Difficulty: ☆☆☆☆☆

Relish: ☆☆☆☆☆

Memories: ☆☆☆☆☆

Notes: ....

....

STOB COIRE SGRIODAIN

Region	Area	Height
Loch Arkaig to Glen Moriston	Highland	979 M / 3212 FEET

Date: ....

Munro order: ....

Duration: ....

Summit time: ....

Distance covered: ....

Start time: ___:___   Finish time: ___:___

Companions: ....
....
....

Rating
Difficulty: ☆☆☆☆☆
Relish: ☆☆☆☆☆
Memories: ☆☆☆☆☆

Weather condition:
☀ ⛅ ☁ 🌧 ⛈ 🌨

PICTURE HERE

Notes: ....
....

BEINN A' CHOCHUILL

Region	Area	Height
Glen Etive to Glen Lochy	Argyll and Bute	980 M / 3215 FEET

Date: .... Munro order: ....

Duration: .... Summit time: ....

Distance covered: .... Start time: ___:___   Finish time: ___:___

Companions: ....

....

Weather condition: ☀ ⛅ 🌥 🌧 ⛈ 🌨

Rating
Difficulty: ☆☆☆☆☆
Relish: ☆☆☆☆☆
Memories: ☆☆☆☆☆

Notes: ....
....

MAOL CHINN-DEARG

Region	Area	Height
Glen Shiel to Loch Hourn and Loch Quoich	Highland	980.3 M /3216 FEET

Date: .... Munro order: ....

Duration: .... Summit time: ....

Distance covered: .... Start time: ___:___   Finish time: ___:___

Companions: ....

....

— Weather condition: —

☀ ⛅ ☁ 🌧 ⛈ 🌨

— Rating —

Difficulty: ☆☆☆☆☆
Relish: ☆☆☆☆☆
Memories: ☆☆☆☆☆

PICTURE HERE

Notes: ....
....

III

MEALL NA AIGHEAN

Region	Area	Height
Loch Rannoch to Glen Lyon	Perth and Kinross	981 M /3219 FEET

Date: .... Munro order: ....

Duration: .... Summit time: ....

Distance covered: .... Start time: ___:___   Finish time: ___:___

Companions: ....

....

Weather condition: ☀ ⛅ ☁ 🌧 ⛈ 🌨

Rating
Difficulty: ☆☆☆☆☆
Relish: ☆☆☆☆☆
Memories: ☆☆☆☆☆

Notes: ....
....

SLIOCH

Region	Area	Height
Loch Rannoch to Glen Lyon	Perth and Kinross	981 M /3219 FEET

Date: .... Munro order: ....

Duration: .... Summit time: ....

Distance covered: .... Start time: ___:___   Finish time: ___:___

Companions: ....

....

....

——— Weather condition: ———

☐ ☀ ☐ ⛅ ☐ ☁ ☐ 🌧 ☐ ⛈ ☐ 🌨

——— Rating ———

Difficulty: ☆ ☆ ☆ ☆ ☆

Relish: ☆ ☆ ☆ ☆ ☆

Memories: ☆ ☆ ☆ ☆ ☆

Notes: ....

....

CISTE DHUBH

Region	Area	Height
Loch Duich to Cannich	Highland	981.1 M / 3219 FEET

Date: ....

Duration: ....

Distance covered: ....

Companions: ....
....
....

Munro order: ....

Summit time: ....

Start time: ___:___   Finish time: ___:___

— Rating —

Difficulty: ☆☆☆☆☆

Relish: ☆☆☆☆☆

Memories: ☆☆☆☆☆

— Weather condition: —
☼ ⛅ ☁ 🌧 ⛈ ❄

Notes: ....
....

STOB COIRE A' CHAIRN

Region	Area	Height
The Fannaichs	Highland	981.3 M / 3219 FEET

Date: .... Munro order: ....

Duration: .... Summit time: ....

Distance covered: .... Start time: ___:___   Finish time: ___:___

Companions: ....
....
....

— Weather condition: —
☀ ⛅ 🌥 🌧 ⛈ 🌨

— Rating —
Difficulty: ☆ ☆ ☆ ☆ ☆
Relish: ☆ ☆ ☆ ☆ ☆
Memories: ☆ ☆ ☆ ☆ ☆

PICTURE HERE

Notes: ....
....

AN GEARANACH

Region	Area	Height
Fort Wiliam to Loch Treig & Loch Leven	Highland	936 M / 3220 FEET

Date: .... Munro order: ....

Duration: .... Summit time: ....

Distance covered: .... Start time: ___:___   Finish time: ___:___

Companions: ....

....

Weather condition: ☐ ☀ ☐ ⛅ ☐ ☁ ☐ 🌧 ☐ ⛈ ☐ 🌨

Rating
Difficulty: ☆☆☆☆☆
Relish: ☆☆☆☆☆
Memories: ☆☆☆☆☆

Notes: ....

....

116

MULLACH NA DHEIRAGAIN

Region	Area	Height
Loch Duich to Cannich	Highland	982 M /3222 FEET

Date: .... Munro order: ....

Duration: .... Summit time: ....

Distance covered: .... Start time: ___:___   Finish time: ___:___

Companions: ....
....
....

— Weather condition: —

☀ ⛅ ☁ 🌧 ⛈ 🌨

— Rating —

Difficulty: ☆☆☆☆☆
Relish: ☆☆☆☆☆
Memories: ☆☆☆☆☆

PICTURE HERE

Notes: ....
....

BEN VORLICH

Region	Area	Height
Strathyre to Strathallan	Perth and Kinross	985 M /3232 FEET

Date: .... Munro order: ....

Duration: .... Summit time: ....

Distance covered: .... Start time: ___:___   Finish time: ___:___

Companions: ....

....

—— Weather condition: ——   —— Rating ——

Difficulty: ☆☆☆☆☆

Relish: ☆☆☆☆☆

Memories: ☆☆☆☆☆

Notes: ....
....

SGURR DEARG

Region	Area	Height
Loch Arkaig to Glen Moriston	Highland	985.8 M / 3235 FEET

Date: .... Munro order: ....

Duration: .... Summit time: ....

Distance covered: .... Start time: ___:___   Finish time: ___:___

Companions: ....
....

────── Weather condition: ──────

☐ ☀ ☐ ⛅ ☐ ☁ ☐ 🌧 ☐ ⛈ ☐ 🌨

────── Rating ──────

Difficulty: ☆ ☆ ☆ ☆ ☆
Relish: ☆ ☆ ☆ ☆ ☆
Memories: ☆ ☆ ☆ ☆ ☆

Notes: ....
....

BEINN ALLIGIN
SGURR MHOR

Region	Area	Height
Loch Torridon to Loch Maree	Highland	986 M /3235 FEET

Date: .... Munro order: ....

Duration: .... Summit time: ....

Distance covered: .... Start time: ___:___   Finish time: ___:___

Companions: ....
....

Weather condition:

Rating
Difficulty: ☆☆☆☆☆
Relish: ☆☆☆☆☆
Memories: ☆☆☆☆☆

Notes: ....
....

DRUIM SHIONNACH

Region	Area	Height
Glen Shiel to Loch Hourn and Loch Quoich	Highland	987 M / 3238 FEET

Date: .... Munro order: ....

Duration: .... Summit time: ....

Distance covered: .... Start time: ___:___   Finish time: ___:___

Companions: ....
....

— Weather condition: —

☀ ⛅ ☁ 🌧 ⛈ 🌨

— Rating —

Difficulty: ☆☆☆☆☆
Relish: ☆☆☆☆☆
Memories: ☆☆☆☆☆

PICTURE HERE

Notes: ....
....

GAOR BHEINN

Region	Area	Height
Mallaig to Fort William	Highland	987 M /3238FEET

Date: .... Munro order: ....

Duration: .... Summit time: ....

Distance covered: .... Start time: ___:___   Finish time: ___:___

Companions: ....
....
....

── Weather condition: ──   ── Rating ──

Difficulty: ☆ ☆ ☆ ☆ ☆

Relish: ☆ ☆ ☆ ☆ ☆

Memories: ☆ ☆ ☆ ☆ ☆

Notes: ....
....

LURG MHOR

Region	Area	Height
Kyle of Lochalsh to Garve	Highland	987 M / 3238 FEET

Date: ....

Duration: ....

Distance covered: ....

Companions: ....
....
....

Munro order: ....

Summit time: ....

Start time: ___:___   Finish time: ___:___

Rating

Difficulty: ☆ ☆ ☆ ☆ ☆

Relish: ☆ ☆ ☆ ☆ ☆

Memories: ☆ ☆ ☆ ☆ ☆

Weather condition:

Notes: ....
....

CONIVAL

Region	Area	Height
Scourie to Lairg	Highland	987 M /3238 FEET

Date: .... Munro order: ....

Duration: .... Summit time: ....

Distance covered: .... Start time: ___:___   Finish time: ___:___

Companions: ....

....

Weather condition:
☀️ ☁️ 🌥️ 🌧️ ⛈️ 🌨️

Rating
Difficulty: ☆☆☆☆☆
Relish: ☆☆☆☆☆
Memories: ☆☆☆☆☆

Notes: ....
....

CREAG LEACACH

Region	Area	Height
Braemar to Montrose	Angus /Perth and Kinross	988.2 M /3242 FEET

Date: .... Munro order: ....

Duration: .... Summit time: ....

Distance covered: .... Start time: ___:___   Finish time: ___:___

Companions: ....
....
....

— Weather condition: —

— Rating —

Difficulty: ☆☆☆☆☆
Relish: ☆☆☆☆☆
Memories: ☆☆☆☆☆

PICTURE HERE

Notes: ....
....

BEINN EUNAICH

Region	Area	Height
Glen Etive to Glen Lochy	Argyll and Bute	989 M /3245 FEET

Date: ....

Munro order: ....

Duration: ....

Summit time: ....

Distance covered: ....

Start time: ___:___   Finish time: ___:___

Companions: ....

....

....

— Weather condition: —

— Rating —

Difficulty: ☆☆☆☆☆

Relish: ☆☆☆☆☆

Memories: ☆☆☆☆☆

Notes: ....
....

SGURR BAN

Region	Area	Height
Loch Maree to Loch Broom	Highland	989 M / 3245 FEET

Date: .... Munro order: ....

Duration: .... Summit time: ....

Distance covered: .... Start time: ___:___   Finish time: ___:___

Companions: ....

....

Weather condition: ☀ ⛅ ☁ 🌧 ⛈ 🌨

Rating
Difficulty: ☆☆☆☆☆
Relish: ☆☆☆☆☆
Memories: ☆☆☆☆☆

Notes: ....

SGAIRNEACH MHOR

Region	Area	Height
Loch Ericht to Glen Tromie & Glen Garry	Perth and Kinross	991 M / 3251 FEET

Date: ....

Munro order: ....

Duration: ....

Summit time: ....

Distance covered: ....

Start time: ___:___   Finish time: ___:___

Companions: ....
....
....

Rating

Difficulty: ☆ ☆ ☆ ☆ ☆

Relish: ☆ ☆ ☆ ☆ ☆

Memories: ☆ ☆ ☆ ☆ ☆

Weather condition:
☐ ☀ ☐ ⛅ ☐ ☁ ☐ 🌧 ☐ ⛈ ☐ 🌨

Notes: ....
....

CARN NAN GOBHAR

Region	Area	Height
Kyle of Lochalsh to Garve	Highland	992 M /3255 FEET

Date: ....

Munro order: ....

Duration: ....

Summit time: ....

Distance covered: ....

Start time: ___:___   Finish time: ___:___

Companions: ....
....
....

Rating

Difficulty: ☆☆☆☆☆

Relish: ☆☆☆☆☆

Memories: ☆☆☆☆☆

Weather condition:
☀ ⛅ ☁ 🌧 ⛈ 🌨

Notes: ....
....

SGURR ALASDAR

Region	Area	Height
Minginish and the Cuillin Hills	Highland	992 M /3255 FEET

Date: .... Munro order: ....

Duration: .... Summit time: ....

Distance covered: .... Start time: ___:___   Finish time: ___:___

Companions: ....

....

Weather condition: ☀ ⛅ ☁ 🌧 ⛈ 🌨

Rating
Difficulty: ☆☆☆☆☆
Relish: ☆☆☆☆☆
Memories: ☆☆☆☆☆

Notes: ....

SGURR NA RUAIDHE

Region	Area	Height
Loch Arkaig to Glen Moriston	Highland	993 M / 3258 FEET

Date: ....

Munro order: ....

Duration: ....

Summit time: ....

Distance covered: ....

Start time: ___:___   Finish time: ___:___

Companions: ....

....

....

Rating

Difficulty: ☆☆☆☆☆

Relish: ☆☆☆☆☆

Memories: ☆☆☆☆☆

Weather condition:

☀ ⛅ ☁ 🌧 ⛈ 🌨

PICTURE HERE

Notes: ....

....

CARN NAN GOBHAR

Region	Area	Height
Killian to Inverness	Highland	993 M /3258 FEET

Date: .... Munro order: ....

Duration: .... Summit time: ....

Distance covered: .... Start time: ___:___   Finish time: ___:___

Companions: ....

....

Rating

Difficulty: ☆ ☆ ☆ ☆ ☆

Relish: ☆ ☆ ☆ ☆ ☆

Memories: ☆ ☆ ☆ ☆ ☆

Weather condition: ☀ ⛅ ☁ 🌧 ⛈ 🌨

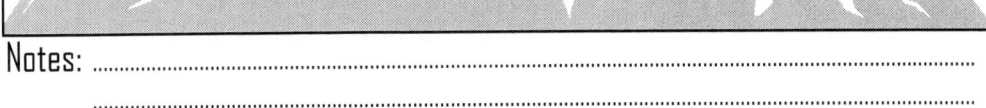

PICTURE HERE

Notes: ....

....

BEINN EIGHE
SPIDEAN COIRE NAN CLACH

Region	Area	Height
Loch Torridon to Loch Maree	Highland	993 M / 3258 FEET

Date: ....

Munro order: ....

Duration: ....

Summit time: ....

Distance covered: ....

Start time: ___:___   Finish time: ___:___

Companions: ....
....

Rating

Difficulty: ☆ ☆ ☆ ☆ ☆

Relish: ☆ ☆ ☆ ☆ ☆

Memories: ☆ ☆ ☆ ☆ ☆

Weather condition:
☐ ☀ ☐ ⛅ ☐ ☁ ☐ 🌧 ☐ ⛈ ☐ 🌨

Notes: ....
....

CARN AN FHIDHLEIR

Region	Area	Height
Glen Tromie to Glen Tilt		994 M /3261 FEET

Date: .... Munro order: ....

Duration: .... Summit time: ....

Distance covered: .... Start time: ___:___   Finish time: ___:___

Companions: ....
....

Weather condition: ☀ ⛅ ☁ 🌧 ⛈ 🌨

Rating
Difficulty: ☆☆☆☆☆
Relish: ☆☆☆☆☆
Memories: ☆☆☆☆☆

Notes: ....
....

SGURR NA H-ULAIDH

Region	Area	Height
Loch Arkaig to Glen Moriston	Highland	994 M /3261 FEET

Date: ....

Duration: ....

Distance covered: ....

Companions: ....
....
....

Munro order: ....

Summit time: ....

Start time: ___:___   Finish time: ___:___

─── Rating ───

Difficulty: ☆ ☆ ☆ ☆ ☆

Relish: ☆ ☆ ☆ ☆ ☆

Memories: ☆ ☆ ☆ ☆ ☆

─── Weather condition: ───

☐ ☐ ☐ ☐ ☐ ☐

Notes: ....
....

AN CAISTEAL

Region	Area	Height
Loch Lomond to Strathyre	Stirling	995.9 M / 3267 FEET

Date: .... Munro order: ....

Duration: .... Summit time: ....

Distance covered: .... Start time: ___:___   Finish time: ___:___

Companions: ....
....
....

Rating
Difficulty: ☆☆☆☆☆
Relish: ☆☆☆☆☆
Memories: ☆☆☆☆☆

Weather condition:
☐ ☀ ☐ ⛅ ☐ ☁ ☐ 🌧 ☐ ⛈ ☐ 🌨

Notes: ....
....

136

SPIDEAN MIALACH

Region	Area	Height
Loch Arkaig to Glen Moriston	Highland	996 M / 3268 FEET

Date: ....

Duration: ....

Distance covered: ....

Companions: ....
....
....

Munro order: ....

Summit time: ....

Start time: ___:___   Finish time: ___:___

Rating

Difficulty: ☆ ☆ ☆ ☆ ☆

Relish: ☆ ☆ ☆ ☆ ☆

Memories: ☆ ☆ ☆ ☆ ☆

Weather condition:
☀ ⛅ ☁ 🌧 ⛈ 🌨

Notes: ....
....

A' CHAILLEACH

Region	Area	Height
The Fannaichs	Highland	997 M / 3271 FEET

Date: .... Munro order: ....

Duration: .... Summit time: ....

Distance covered: .... Start time: ___:___ Finish time: ___:___

Companions: ....

....

— Weather condition: —

☀ ⛅ ☁ 🌧 ⛈ 🌨

— Rating —

Difficulty: ☆☆☆☆☆
Relish: ☆☆☆☆☆
Memories: ☆☆☆☆☆

Notes: ....
....

GLAS BHEINN MHOR

Region	Area	Height
Glen Etive to Glen Lochy	Argyll and Bute /Highland	997.7 M /3273 FEET

Date: .... Munro order: ....

Duration: .... Summit time: ....

Distance covered: .... Start time: ___:___   Finish time: ___:___

Companions: ....

────────── Weather condition: ──────────

☐ ☀ ☐ ⛅ ☐ ☁ ☐ 🌧 ☐ ⛈ ☐ 🌨

─ Rating ─
Difficulty: ☆ ☆ ☆ ☆ ☆
Relish: ☆ ☆ ☆ ☆ ☆
Memories: ☆ ☆ ☆ ☆ ☆

PICTURE HERE

Notes: ....
....

BROAD CAIRN

Region	Area	Height
Braemar to Montrose	Aberdeenshire /Angus	998 M /3274 FEET

Date: .... Munro order: ....

Duration: .... Summit time: ....

Distance covered: .... Start time: ___:___   Finish time: ___:___

Companions: ....

— Weather condition: —

— Rating —

Difficulty: ☆☆☆☆☆

Relish: ☆☆☆☆☆

Memories: ☆☆☆☆☆

Notes: ....

BEN MORE ASSYNT

Region	Area	Height
Scourie to Lairg	Highland	998 M /3274 FEET

Date: .... Munro order: ....

Duration: .... Summit time: ....

Distance covered: .... Start time: ___:___   Finish time: ___:___

Companions: ....

....

....

— Weather condition: —

☐ ☀   ☐ ⛅   ☐ ☁   ☐ 🌧   ☐ ⛈   ☐ 🌨

— Rating —

Difficulty: ☆ ☆ ☆ ☆ ☆

Relish: ☆ ☆ ☆ ☆ ☆

Memories: ☆ ☆ ☆ ☆ ☆

PICTURE HERE

Notes: ....

....

SGURR BREAC

Region	Area	Height
The Fannaichs	Highland	999 M /3278 FEET

Date: ....

Munro order: ....

Duration: ....

Summit time: ....

Distance covered: ....

Start time: ___:___   Finish time: ___:___

Companions: ....
....
....

Rating
Difficulty: ☆☆☆☆☆
Relish: ☆☆☆☆☆
Memories: ☆☆☆☆☆

Weather condition: ☀️ ⛅ ☁️ 🌧️ ⛈️ 🌨️

PICTURE HERE

Notes: ....
....

SAIL CHAORAINN

Region	Area	Height
Glen Affric to Glen Moriston	Highland	999.2 M / 3278 FEET

Date: .... Munro order: ....

Duration: .... Summit time: ....

Distance covered: .... Start time: ___:___   Finish time: ___:___

Companions: ....
....

— Weather condition: —

— Rating —
Difficulty: ☆☆☆☆☆
Relish: ☆☆☆☆☆
Memories: ☆☆☆☆☆

Notes: ....
....

STOB DAIMH

Region	Area	Height
The Fannaichs	Highland	999.2 M / 3278 FEET

Date: .... Munro order: ....

Duration: .... Summit time: ....

Distance covered: .... Start time: ___:___   Finish time: ___:___

Companions: ....

....

Weather condition:

☀ ⛅ 🌥 🌧 ⛈ 🌨

Rating

Difficulty: ☆☆☆☆☆
Relish: ☆☆☆☆☆
Memories: ☆☆☆☆☆

Notes: ....
....

SGURR CHOINNICH

Region	Area	Height
Loch Arkaig to Glen Moriston	Highland	999.2 M /3008 FEET

Date: ....

Munro order: ....

Duration: ....

Summit time: ....

Distance covered: ....

Start time: ___:___   Finish time: ___:___

Companions: ....
....
....

— Weather condition: —
☀ ⛅ ☁ 🌧 ⛈ 🌨

— Rating —
Difficulty: ☆ ☆ ☆ ☆ ☆
Relish: ☆ ☆ ☆ ☆ ☆
Memories: ☆ ☆ ☆ ☆ ☆

PICTURE HERE

Notes: ....
....

STOB BAN

Region	Area	Height
Loch Arkaig to Glen Moriston	Highland	999.7 M /3280 FEET

Date: .... Munro order: ....

Duration: .... Summit time: ....

Distance covered: .... Start time: ___:___   Finish time: ___:___

Companions: ....
....
....

Weather condition:
☐ ☀ ☐ ⛅ ☐ ☁ ☐ 🌧 ☐ ⛈ ☐ 🌨

Rating
Difficulty: ☆☆☆☆☆
Relish: ☆☆☆☆☆
Memories: ☆☆☆☆☆

Notes: ....
....

MEALL GREIGH

Region	Area	Height
Glen Lyon to Glen Dochart & Loch Tay	Perth and Kinross	1001 M /3284 FEET

Date: .... Munro order: ....

Duration: .... Summit time: ....

Distance covered: .... Start time: ___:___   Finish time: ___:___

Companions: ....

....

— Weather condition: —

☀ ⛅ 🌥 🌧 ⛈ 🌨

— Rating —

Difficulty: ☆ ☆ ☆ ☆ ☆

Relish: ☆ ☆ ☆ ☆ ☆

Memories: ☆ ☆ ☆ ☆ ☆

PICTURE HERE

Notes: ....

....

BEINN A' BHEITHIR
SGORR DHONULL

Region	Area	Height
Loch Linnhe to Loch Etive	Highland	1001 M / 3284 FEET

Date: .... Munro order: ....

Duration: .... Summit time: ....

Distance covered: .... Start time: ___:___   Finish time: ___:___

Companions: ....
....
....

Weather condition:
☀️ ⛅ ☁️ 🌧️ ⛈️ 🌨️

Rating
Difficulty: ☆☆☆☆☆
Relish: ☆☆☆☆☆
Memories: ☆☆☆☆☆

Notes: ....
....

AONACH MEADHOIN

Region	Area	Height
Loch Duich to Cannich	Highland	1001 M /3284 FEET

Date: .... Munro order: ....

Duration: .... Summit time: ....

Distance covered: .... Start time: ___:___   Finish time: ___:___

Companions: ....

── Weather condition: ──

── Rating ──
Difficulty: ☆ ☆ ☆ ☆ ☆
Relish: ☆ ☆ ☆ ☆ ☆
Memories: ☆ ☆ ☆ ☆ ☆

Notes: ....

SGURR NA CARNACH

Region	Area	Height
Loch Rannoch to Glen Lyon	Perth and Kinross	1002 M /3287 FEET

Date: ....

Munro order: ....

Duration: ....

Summit time: ....

Distance covered: ....

Start time: ___:___   Finish time: ___:___

Companions: ....
....
....

Rating
Difficulty: ☆☆☆☆☆
Relish: ☆☆☆☆☆
Memories: ☆☆☆☆☆

Weather condition:
☐ ☀ ☐ ⛅ ☐ ☁ ☐ 🌧 ☐ ⛈ ☐ 🌨

PICTURE HERE

Notes: ....
....

SGURR MOR

Region	Area	Height
Loch Arkaig to Glen Moriston	Highland	1003 M /3291 FEET

Date: ....

Munro order: ....

Duration: ....

Summit time: ....

Distance covered: ....

Start time: ___:___   Finish time: ___:___

Companions: ....
....
....

— Weather condition: —
☀ ⛅ ☁ 🌧 ⛈ ❄

— Rating —
Difficulty: ☆☆☆☆☆
Relish: ☆☆☆☆☆
Memories: ☆☆☆☆☆

PICTURE HERE

Notes: ....
....

BEINN AN DOTHAIDH

Region	Area	Height
Loch Rannoch to Glen Lyon	Argyll and Bute	936 M /3220 FEET

Date: .... Munro order: ....

Duration: .... Summit time: ....

Distance covered: .... Start time: ___:___   Finish time: ___:___

Companions: ....

....

— Weather condition: —

☀ ⛅ 🌥 🌧 ⛈ 🌨

— Rating —

Difficulty: ☆☆☆☆☆

Relish: ☆☆☆☆☆

Memories: ☆☆☆☆☆

PICTURE HERE

Notes: ....

....

SGURR AN LOCHAIN

Region	Area	Height
Glen Shiel to Loch Hourn and Loch Quoich	Highland	1004 M /3294 FEET

Date: ....

Duration: ....

Distance covered: ....

Companions: ....
....
....

Weather condition:
☐ ☀ ☐ ⛅ ☐ ☁ ☐ 🌧 ☐ ⛈ ☐ 🌨

Munro order: ....

Summit time: ....

Start time: ___:___   Finish time: ___:___

Rating
Difficulty: ☆ ☆ ☆ ☆ ☆
Relish: ☆ ☆ ☆ ☆ ☆
Memories: ☆ ☆ ☆ ☆ ☆

PICTURE HERE

Notes: ....
....

BEINN FHIONNLAIDH

Region	Area	Height
Loch Linnhe to Loch Etive	Argyll and Bute	959 M / 3146 FEET

Date: ....

Munro order: ....

Duration: ....

Summit time: ....

Distance covered: ....

Start time: ___:___   Finish time: ___:___

Companions: ....

....

....

Rating

Difficulty: ☆☆☆☆☆

Relish: ☆☆☆☆☆

Memories: ☆☆☆☆☆

Weather condition:

☀ ⛅ ☁ 🌧 ⛈ 🌨

PICTURE HERE

Notes: ....

....

MAOILE LUNDAIDH

Region	Area	Height
Kyle of Lochlash to Garve	Highland	1004.9 M /3297 FEET

Date: ....

Munro order: ....

Duration: ....

Summit time: ....

Distance covered: ....

Start time: ___:___   Finish time: ___:___

Companions: ....
....
....

Rating

Difficulty: ☆☆☆☆☆

Relish: ☆☆☆☆☆

Memories: ☆☆☆☆☆

Weather condition:
☐ ☐ ☐ ☐ ☐ ☐

PICTURE HERE

Notes: ....
....

CARN LIATH

Region	Area	Height
Loach Lochy to Loach Laggan	Highland	1006 M /3301 FEET

Date: ....   Munro order: ....

Duration: ....   Summit time: ....

Distance covered: ....   Start time: ___:___   Finish time: ___:___

Companions: ....
....
....

— Weather condition: —

☀ ⛅ ☁ 🌧 ⛈ 🌨

— Rating —

Difficulty: ☆ ☆ ☆ ☆ ☆
Relish: ☆ ☆ ☆ ☆ ☆
Memories: ☆ ☆ ☆ ☆ ☆

Notes: ....
....

AN SGARSOCH

Region	Area	Height
Glen Tromie to Glen Tilt	Aberdeenshire /Perth and Kinross	1006.5 M /3302 FEET

Date: .... Munro order: ....

Duration: .... Summit time: ....

Distance covered: .... Start time: ___:___   Finish time: ___:___

Companions: ....
....
....

— Weather condition: —

— Rating —

Difficulty: ☆☆☆☆☆
Relish: ☆☆☆☆☆
Memories: ☆☆☆☆☆

PICTURE HERE

Notes: ....
....

THE DEVIL'S POINT

Region	Area	Height
The Fannaichs	Highland	1006.9 M /3303 FEET

Date: ....

Munro order: ....

Duration: ....

Summit time: ....

Distance covered: ....

Start time: ___:___   Finish time: ___:___

Companions: ....
....
....

Weather condition:
- ☐ ☀
- ☐ ⛅
- ☐ ☁
- ☐ 🌧
- ☐ ⛈
- ☐ 🌨

Rating
- Difficulty: ☆☆☆☆☆
- Relish: ☆☆☆☆☆
- Memories: ☆☆☆☆☆

PICTURE HERE

Notes: ....
....

BEINN DEARG

Region	Area	Height
Glen Tromie to Glen Tilt	Perth and Kinros	1008.7 M / 3309 FEET

Date: ....

Munro order: ....

Duration: ....

Summit time: ....

Distance covered: ....

Start time: ___:___   Finish time: ___:___

Companions: ....
....

Rating
Difficulty: ☆☆☆☆☆
Relish: ☆☆☆☆☆
Memories: ☆☆☆☆☆

Weather condition:
☐ ☀ ☐ ⛅ ☐ ☁ ☐ 🌧 ☐ ⛈ ☐ 🌨

Notes: ....
....

BEINN EIGHE
RUADH-STAC MOR

Region	Area	Height
Loch Torridon to Loch Maree	Highland	1010 M / 3314 FEET

Date: .... Munro order: ....

Duration: .... Summit time: ....

Distance covered: .... Start time: ___:___   Finish time: ___:___

Companions: ....

....

Weather condition:
☐ ☀ ☐ ⛅ ☐ ☁ ☐ 🌧 ☐ ⛈ ☐ 🌨

Rating
Difficulty: ☆☆☆☆☆
Relish: ☆☆☆☆☆
Memories: ☆☆☆☆☆

Notes: ....

....

SGURR AN DOIRE LEATHAIN

Region	Area	Height
Glen Shiel to Loch Hourn and Loch Quoich	Highland	1,010 M / 3314 FEET

Date: .... Munro order: ....

Duration: .... Summit time: ....

Distance covered: .... Start time: ___:___   Finish time: ___:___

Companions: ....

....

....

Weather condition: ☀ ⛅ ☁ 🌧 ⛈ 🌨

Rating
Difficulty: ☆☆☆☆☆
Relish: ☆☆☆☆☆
Memories: ☆☆☆☆☆

Notes: ....
....

SGURR EILDE MOR

Region	Area	Height
Loch Arkaig to Glen Moriston	Highland	1010 M / 3314 FEET

Date: .... Munro order: ....

Duration: .... Summit time: ....

Distance covered: .... Start time: ___:___   Finish time: ___:___

Companions: ....

....

Weather condition: ☐ ☀️ ☐ 🌤️ ☐ ☁️ ☐ 🌧️ ☐ ⛈️ ☐ 🌨️

Rating
Difficulty: ☆☆☆☆☆
Relish: ☆☆☆☆☆
Memories: ☆☆☆☆☆

Notes: ....

....

BEINN UDLAMAIN

Region	Area	Height
Loch Ericht to Glen Tromie & Glen Garry	Highland / Perth and Kinross	1010.2 M / 3314 FEET

Date: .... Munro order: ....

Duration: .... Summit time: ....

Distance covered: .... Start time: ___:___   Finish time: ___:___

Companions: ....
....
....

— Rating —
Difficulty: ☆ ☆ ☆ ☆ ☆
Relish: ☆ ☆ ☆ ☆ ☆
Memories: ☆ ☆ ☆ ☆ ☆

— Weather condition: —
☀ ⛅ 🌥 🌧 ⛈ 🌨

Notes: ....
....

THE SADDLE

Region	Area	Height
Loch Arkaig to Glen Moriston	Highland	1011.4 M / 3318 FEET

Date: .... Munro order: ....

Duration: .... Summit time: ....

Distance covered: .... Start time: ___:___   Finish time: ___:___

Companions: ....

....

Weather condition: ☀ ⛅ ☁ 🌧 ⛈ 🌨

Rating
- Difficulty: ☆☆☆☆☆
- Relish: ☆☆☆☆☆
- Memories: ☆☆☆☆☆

Notes: ....

CAIRN BANNOCH

Region	Area	Height
Braemar to Montrose	Highland	1012 M / 3320 FEET

Date: ....

Munro order: ....

Duration: ....

Summit time: ....

Distance covered: ....

Start time: ___:___   Finish time: ___:___

Companions: ....
....

— Rating —

Difficulty: ☆ ☆ ☆ ☆ ☆

Relish: ☆ ☆ ☆ ☆ ☆

Memories: ☆ ☆ ☆ ☆ ☆

— Weather condition: —

☐ ☐ ☐ ☐ ☐ ☐

Notes: ....
....

BEINN IME

Region	Area	Height
Inveraray to Crianlarich	Argyll and Bute	1012.2 M /3321 FEET

Date: .... Munro order: ....

Duration: .... Summit time: ....

Distance covered: .... Start time: ___:___   Finish time: ___:___

Companions: ....

....

Weather condition:
☐ ☀ ☐ ⛅ ☐ 🌥 ☐ 🌧 ☐ ⛈ ☐ 🌨

Rating
Difficulty: ☆☆☆☆☆
Relish: ☆☆☆☆☆
Memories: ☆☆☆☆☆

Notes: ....
....

GARBH CHIOCH MHOR

Region	Area	Height
Knoydart to Glen Kingie	Highland	1012.9 M / 3323 FEET

Date: ....

Munro order: ....

Duration: ....

Summit time: ....

Distance covered: ....

Start time: ___:___   Finish time: ___:___

Companions: ....
....

Weather condition:
☀️ ⛅ ☁️ 🌧️ ⛈️ 🌨️

Rating
Difficulty: ☆☆☆☆☆
Relish: ☆☆☆☆☆
Memories: ☆☆☆☆☆

PICTURE HERE

Notes: ....
....

MULLACH COIRE MHIC FHEARCHAIR

Region	Area	Height
Loch Maree to Loch Broom	Highland	1015.2 M / 3331 FEET

Date: .... Munro order: ....

Duration: .... Summit time: ....

Distance covered: .... Start time: ___:___   Finish time: ___:___

Companions: ....

——— Rating ———

Difficulty: ☆☆☆☆☆

Relish: ☆☆☆☆☆

Memories: ☆☆☆☆☆

——— Weather condition: ———

☀ ⛅ 🌥 🌧 ⛈ 🌨

Notes: ....

MULLACH CLACH A' BHLAIR

Region	Area	Height
Cairngorms	Highland	1019 M / 3343 FEET

Date: .... Munro order: ....

Duration: .... Summit time: ....

Distance covered: .... Start time: ___:___   Finish time: ___:___

Companions: ....
....
....

Weather condition: ☀ ⛅ ☁ 🌧 ⛈ 🌨

Rating
Difficulty: ☆☆☆☆☆
Relish: ☆☆☆☆☆
Memories: ☆☆☆☆☆

PICTURE HERE

Notes: ....
....

CARN AN TUIRC

Region	Area	Height
Braemar to Montrose	Aberdeenshire	1019 M / 3343 FEET

Date: .... Munro order: ....

Duration: .... Summit time: ....

Distance covered: .... Start time: ___:___   Finish time: ___:___

Companions: ....

....

....

Weather condition: ☐ ☐ ☐ ☐ ☐ ☐

Rating

Difficulty: ☆ ☆ ☆ ☆ ☆

Relish: ☆ ☆ ☆ ☆ ☆

Memories: ☆ ☆ ☆ ☆ ☆

PICTURE HERE

Notes: ....

BEINN BHEOIL

Region	Area	Height
Loch Treig to Loch Ericht	Highland	1019 M /3343 FEET

Date: .... Munro order: ....

Duration: .... Summit time: ....

Distance covered: .... Start time: ___:___   Finish time: ___:___

Companions: ....
....

— Weather condition: —

☀ ⛅ ☁ 🌧 ⛈ 🌨

— Rating —

Difficulty: ☆ ☆ ☆ ☆ ☆

Relish: ☆ ☆ ☆ ☆ ☆

Memories: ☆ ☆ ☆ ☆ ☆

PICTURE HERE

Notes: ....
....

AONACH AIR CHRITH

Region	Area	Height
Glen Shiel to Loch Hourn and Loch Quoich	Highland	1019.5 M /3345 FEET

Date: .... Munro order: ....

Duration: .... Summit time: ....

Distance covered: .... Start time: ___:___   Finish time: ___:___

Companions: ....
....

— Weather condition: —
☐ ☀️ ☐ ⛅ ☐ 🌥️ ☐ 🌧️ ☐ ⛈️ ☐ 🌨️

— Rating —
Difficulty: ☆☆☆☆☆
Relish: ☆☆☆☆☆
Memories: ☆☆☆☆☆

PICTURE HERE

Notes: ....
....

LADHAR BHEINN

Region	Area	Height
Knoydart to Glen Kingie	Highland	1020 M / 3346 FEET

Date: ....

Duration: ....

Distance covered: ....

Companions: ....
....
....

Munro order: ....

Summit time: ....

Start time: ___:___   Finish time: ___:___

— Weather condition: —

— Rating —

Difficulty: ☆ ☆ ☆ ☆ ☆

Relish: ☆ ☆ ☆ ☆ ☆

Memories: ☆ ☆ ☆ ☆ ☆

Notes: ....
....

BUACHAILLE ETIVE MOR
STOB DEARG

Region	Area	Height
Loch Linnhe to Loch Etive	Highland	1021.4 M / 3351 FEET

Date: .... Munro order: ....

Duration: .... Summit time: ....

Distance covered: .... Start time: ___:___   Finish time: ___:___

Companions: ....
....

Weather condition: ☐ ☀ ☐ ⛅ ☐ ☁ ☐ 🌧 ☐ ⛈ ☐ 🌨

Rating
Difficulty: ☆☆☆☆☆
Relish: ☆☆☆☆☆
Memories: ☆☆☆☆☆

Notes: ....
....

LIATHACH
MULLACH AN RATHAIN

Region	Area	Height
Loch Torridon to Loch Maree	Highland	1023.8 M /3359 FEET

Date: .... Munro order: ....

Duration: .... Summit time: ....

Distance covered: .... Start time: ___:___   Finish time: ___:___

Companions: ....

....

Weather condition: ☀ ⛅ ☁ 🌧 ⛈ 🌨

Rating
Difficulty: ☆☆☆☆☆
Relish: ☆☆☆☆☆
Memories: ☆☆☆☆☆

Notes: ....

....

BEINN A' BHEITHIR
SGORR DHEARG

Region	Area	Height
Loch Linnhe to Loch Etive	Highland	1024 M / 3661 FEET

Date: .... Munro order: ....

Duration: .... Summit time: ....

Distance covered: .... Start time: ___:___   Finish time: ___:___

Companions: ....
....
....

Weather condition:
☀️ ⛅ ☁️ 🌧️ ⛈️ 🌨️

Rating
Difficulty: ☆☆☆☆☆
Relish: ☆☆☆☆☆
Memories: ☆☆☆☆☆

Notes: ....
....

BEN CHALLUM

Region	Area	Height
Glen Lyon to Glen Dochart & Loch Tay	Stirling	1025 M / 3363 FEET

Date: ....

Duration: ....

Distance covered: ....

Companions: ....
....
....

Munro order: ....

Summit time: ....

Start time: ___:___   Finish time: ___:___

Weather condition: ☐ ☀ ☐ ⛅ ☐ 🌥 ☐ 🌧 ☐ ⛈ ☐ 🌨

Rating
- Difficulty: ☆☆☆☆☆
- Relish: ☆☆☆☆☆
- Memories: ☆☆☆☆☆

Notes: ....
....

SGURR NA CISTE DUIBHE

Region	Area	Height
Loch Rannoch to Glen Lyon	Perth and Kinross	1027 M / 3369 FEET

Date: .... Munro order: ....

Duration: .... Summit time: ....

Distance covered: .... Start time: ___:___   Finish time: ___:___

Companions: ....

....

— Weather condition: —

☀ ⛅ 🌥 🌧 ⛈ 🌨

— Rating —

Difficulty: ☆☆☆☆☆

Relish: ☆☆☆☆☆

Memories: ☆☆☆☆☆

PICTURE HERE

Notes: ....

....

SGURR A' MHAORAICH

Region	Area	Height
Glen Shiel to Loch Hourn and Loch Quoich	Highland	1027 M / 3369 FEET

Date: .... Munro order: ....

Duration: .... Summit time: ....

Distance covered: .... Start time: ___:___   Finish time: ___:___

Companions: ....

....

Rating

Difficulty: ☆ ☆ ☆ ☆ ☆

Relish: ☆ ☆ ☆ ☆ ☆

Memories: ☆ ☆ ☆ ☆ ☆

Weather condition: ☐ ☀ ☐ ⛅ ☐ ☁ ☐ 🌧 ☐ ⛈ ☐ 🌨

PICTURE HERE

Notes: ....

....

CARN AN RIGH

Region	Area	Height
Pitlochry to Braemar & Blairgowrie	Perth and Kinross	1029 M / 3376 FEET

Date: .... Munro order: ....

Duration: .... Summit time: ....

Distance covered: .... Start time: ___:___   Finish time: ___:___

Companions: ....

....

....

Weather condition:

Rating

Difficulty: ☆☆☆☆☆

Relish: ☆☆☆☆☆

Memories: ☆☆☆☆☆

Notes: ....

....

CARN GORM

Region	Area	Height
Loach Rannoch to Glen Lyon	Perth and Kinross	1029 M / 3376 FEET

Date: ....

Munro order: ....

Duration: ....

Summit time: ....

Distance covered: ....

Start time: ___:___ Finish time: ___:___

Companions: ....
....

Rating
Difficulty: ☆☆☆☆☆
Relish: ☆☆☆☆☆
Memories: ☆☆☆☆☆

Weather condition:

Notes: ....

BEN OSS

Region	Area	Height
Inveraray to Crianlarich	Stirling	1029 M /3367 FEET

Date: .... Munro order: ....

Duration: .... Summit time: ....

Distance covered: .... Start time: ___:___   Finish time: ___:___

Companions: ....

....

Weather condition:
☐ ☀ ☐ ⛅ ☐ 🌥 ☐ 🌧 ☐ ⛈ ☐ 🌨

Rating
Difficulty: ☆☆☆☆☆
Relish: ☆☆☆☆☆
Memories: ☆☆☆☆☆

Notes: ....
....

AM BODACH

Region	Area	Height
Fort William to Loch Treig & Loch Leven	Highland	1031.8 M /3385 FEET

Date: ....

Duration: ....

Distance covered: ....

Companions: ....
....
....

Munro order: ....

Summit time: ....

Start time: ___:___   Finish time: ___:___

— Weather condition: —
☀ ⛅ ☁ 🌧 ⛈ 🌨

— Rating —
Difficulty: ☆ ☆ ☆ ☆ ☆
Relish: ☆ ☆ ☆ ☆ ☆
Memories: ☆ ☆ ☆ ☆ ☆

PICTURE HERE

Notes: ....
....

BEINN FHADA

Region	Area	Height
Loch Duich to Cannich	Highland	1031.9 M /3385 FEET

Date: .... Munro order: ....

Duration: .... Summit time: ....

Distance covered: .... Start time: ___:___   Finish time: ___:___

Companions: ....

....

— Weather condition: —

☐ ☀ ☐ ⛅ ☐ ☁ ☐ 🌧 ☐ ⛈ ☐ 🌨

— Rating —

Difficulty: ☆☆☆☆☆

Relish: ☆☆☆☆☆

Memories: ☆☆☆☆☆

Notes: ....

....

CARN DEARG

Region	Area	Height
Loch Treig to Loch Ericht	Highland	1034 M / 3392 FEET

Date: ....

Munro order: ....

Duration: ....

Summit time: ....

Distance covered: ....

Start time: ___:___   Finish time: ___:___

Companions: ....
....

Rating

Difficulty: ☆ ☆ ☆ ☆ ☆

Relish: ☆ ☆ ☆ ☆ ☆

Memories: ☆ ☆ ☆ ☆ ☆

Weather condition: ☐ ☀ ☐ ⛅ ☐ ☁ ☐ 🌧 ☐ ⛈ ☐ 🌨

PICTURE HERE

Notes: ....
....

GLEOURAICH

Region	Area	Height
Glen Shiel to Loch Hourn and Loch Quoich	Highland	1035 M / 3396 FEET

Date: .... Munro order: ....

Duration: .... Summit time: ....

Distance covered: .... Start time: ___:___ Finish time: ___:___

Companions: ....
....

Weather condition:
☐ ☀ ☐ ⛅ ☐ 🌫 ☐ 🌧 ☐ ⛈ ☐ 🌨

Rating
Difficulty: ☆☆☆☆☆
Relish: ☆☆☆☆☆
Memories: ☆☆☆☆☆

Notes: ....
....

SGURR A' BHEALAICH DHEIRG

Region	Area	Height
Loch Duich to Cannich	Highland	1036 M / 3399 FEET

Date: .... Munro order: ....

Duration: .... Summit time: ....

Distance covered: .... Start time: ___:___   Finish time: ___:___

Companions: ....

....

— Weather condition: —   — Rating —

☀ ⛅ ☁ 🌧 ⛈ ❄   Difficulty: ☆☆☆☆☆
                                  Relish: ☆☆☆☆☆
                                  Memories: ☆☆☆☆☆

PICTURE HERE

Notes: ....
....

CARN A' MHAIM

Region	Area	Height
Cairngorms	Aberdeenshire	1037 M / 3402 FEET

Date: .... Munro order: ....

Duration: .... Summit time: ....

Distance covered: .... Start time: ___:___   Finish time: ___:___

Companions: ....

....

— Weather condition: —

☐ ☐ ☐ ☐ ☐ ☐

— Rating —

Difficulty: ☆ ☆ ☆ ☆ ☆
Relish: ☆ ☆ ☆ ☆ ☆
Memories: ☆ ☆ ☆ ☆ ☆

Notes: ....

....

BEINN ACHALADAIR

Region	Area	Height
Loch Rannoch to Glen Lyon	Argyll and Bute /Perth and Kinross	1038.6 M /3407 FEET

Date: ....

Duration: ....

Distance covered: ....

Companions: ....
....
....

Munro order: ....

Summit time: ....

Start time: ___:___   Finish time: ___:___

Weather condition:
☀ ⛅ ☁ 🌧 ⛈ 🌨

Rating
Difficulty: ☆☆☆☆☆
Relish: ☆☆☆☆☆
Memories: ☆☆☆☆☆

PICTURE HERE

Notes: ....
....

MEALL GHAORDAIDH

Region	Area	Height
Glen Lyon to Glen Dochart & Loch Tay	Perth and Kinross /Stirling	1039.8 M /3411 FEET

Date: .... Munro order: ....

Duration: .... Summit time: ....

Distance covered: .... Start time: ___:___   Finish time: ___:___

Companions: ....

....

Weather condition:
☀️ ⛅ 🌥️ 🌧️ ⛈️ 🌨️

Rating
Difficulty: ☆☆☆☆☆
Relish: ☆☆☆☆☆
Memories: ☆☆☆☆☆

PICTURE HERE

Notes: ....
....

SGURR NA CICHE

Region	Area	Height
Loch Arkaig to Glen Moriston	Highland	1040.2 M /3413 FEET

Date: ....

Duration: ....

Distance covered: ....

Companions: ....
....

Munro order: ....

Summit time: ....

Start time: ___:___   Finish time: ___:___

— Weather condition: —

— Rating —

Difficulty: ☆☆☆☆☆

Relish: ☆☆☆☆☆

Memories: ☆☆☆☆☆

PICTURE HERE

Notes: ....
....

CARN MAIRG

Region	Area	Height
Loach Rannoch to Glen Lyon	Perth and Kinross	1042 M / 3419 FEET

Date: .... Munro order: ....

Duration: .... Summit time: ....

Distance covered: .... Start time: ___:___   Finish time: ___:___

Companions: ....

....

Weather condition:
☐ ☀️ ☐ 🌤️ ☐ 🌥️ ☐ 🌧️ ☐ ⛈️ ☐ 🌨️

Rating
Difficulty: ☆☆☆☆☆
Relish: ☆☆☆☆☆
Memories: ☆☆☆☆☆

PICTURE HERE

Notes: ....

MEALL NAN TARMACHAN

Region	Area	Height
Glen Lyon to Glen Dochart & Loch Tay	Perth and Kinross	1043.6 M / 3424 FEET

Date: ....

Munro order: ....

Duration: ....

Summit time: ....

Distance covered: ....

Start time: ___:___   Finish time: ___:___

Companions: ....
....
....

— Rating —

Difficulty: ☆ ☆ ☆ ☆ ☆

Relish: ☆ ☆ ☆ ☆ ☆

Memories: ☆ ☆ ☆ ☆ ☆

— Weather condition: —

☐ ☀ ☐ ⛅ ☐ ☁ ☐ 🌧 ☐ ⛈ ☐ 🌨

Notes: ....
....

STOB COIR'AN ALBANNAICH

Region	Area	Height
Loch Arkaig to Glen Moriston	Highland	1044 M / 3425 FEET

Date: .... Munro order: ....

Duration: .... Summit time: ....

Distance covered: .... Start time: ___:___   Finish time: ___:___

Companions: ....

....

Weather condition:
☐ ☀ ☐ ⛅ ☐ 🌥 ☐ 🌧 ☐ ⛈ ☐ 🌨

Rating
Difficulty: ☆ ☆ ☆ ☆ ☆
Relish: ☆ ☆ ☆ ☆ ☆
Memories: ☆ ☆ ☆ ☆ ☆

Notes: ....
....

BEINN IUTHARN MHOR

Region	Area	Height
Ptlochry to Braemar & Blairgowrie	Aberdeenshire /Perth and Kinross	1045 M /3428 FEET

Date: ....

Munro order: ....

Duration: ....

Summit time: ....

Distance covered: ....

Start time: ___:___   Finish time: ___:___

Companions: ....
....

— Rating —

Difficulty: ☆ ☆ ☆ ☆ ☆

Relish: ☆ ☆ ☆ ☆ ☆

Memories: ☆ ☆ ☆ ☆ ☆

— Weather condition: —

☀ ⛅ ☁ 🌧 ⛈ ❄

PICTURE HERE

Notes: ....
....

CRUACH ARDRAIN

Region	Area	Height
Loch Lomond to Strathyre	Stirling	1045.9 M /3431FEET

Date: .... Munro order: ....

Duration: .... Summit time: ....

Distance covered: .... Start time: ___:___   Finish time: ___:___

Companions: ....
....
....

Weather condition:

Rating
- Difficulty: ☆☆☆☆☆
- Relish: ☆☆☆☆☆
- Memories: ☆☆☆☆☆

Notes: ....
....

BEN WYVIS

Region	Area	Height
Loch Vaich to Moray Firth	Highland	1046 M /3432 FEET

Date: ....

Munro order: ....

Duration: ....

Summit time: ....

Distance covered: ....

Start time: ___:___   Finish time: ___:___

Companions: ....

....

....

— Rating —

Difficulty: ☆☆☆☆☆

Relish: ☆☆☆☆☆

Memories: ☆☆☆☆☆

— Weather condition: —

☀ ⛅ ☁ 🌧 ⛈ 🌨

Notes: ....

....

CHNO DEARG

Region	Area	Height
Loch Treig to Loch Ericht	Highland	1046 M / 3432 FEET

Date: .... Munro order: ....

Duration: .... Summit time: ....

Distance covered: .... Start time: ___:___   Finish time: ___:___

Companions: ....

— Weather condition: —   — Rating —

Difficulty: ☆☆☆☆☆

Relish: ☆☆☆☆☆

Memories: ☆☆☆☆☆

Notes: ....

CARN AN T-SAGAIRT MOR

Region	Area	Height
Braemar to Montrose	Aberdeenshire	1047 M / 3435 FEET

Date: .... Munro order: ....

Duration: .... Summit time: ....

Distance covered: .... Start time: ___:___   Finish time: ___:___

Companions: ....

──── Rating ────

Difficulty: ☆ ☆ ☆ ☆ ☆

Relish: ☆ ☆ ☆ ☆ ☆

Memories: ☆ ☆ ☆ ☆ ☆

──── Weather condition: ────

☀ ⛅ ☁ 🌧 ⛈ ❄

Notes: ....

CREAG MHOR

Region	Area	Height
Glen Lyon to Glen Dochart & Loch Tay	Perth and Kinross /Stirling	1047 M /3435FEET

Date: .... Munro order: ....

Duration: .... Summit time: ....

Distance covered: .... Start time: ___:___   Finish time: ___:___

Companions: ....

──── Rating ────

Difficulty: ☆ ☆ ☆ ☆ ☆

Relish: ☆ ☆ ☆ ☆ ☆

Memories: ☆ ☆ ☆ ☆ ☆

── Weather condition: ──

☐ ☀ ☐ ⛅ ☐ ☁ ☐ 🌧 ☐ ⛈ ☐ 🌨

Notes: ....

SGURR FHUAR-THUILL

Region	Area	Height
Loch Rannoch to Glen Lyon	Perth and Kinross	1049 M / 3442 FEET

Date: .... Munro order: ....

Duration: .... Summit time: ....

Distance covered: .... Start time: ___:___   Finish time: ___:___

Companions: ....

....

— Weather condition: —   — Rating —

☐ ☀ ☐ ⛅ ☐ ☁ ☐ 🌧 ☐ ⛈ ☐ 🌨

Difficulty: ☆ ☆ ☆ ☆ ☆

Relish: ☆ ☆ ☆ ☆ ☆

Memories: ☆ ☆ ☆ ☆ ☆

PICTURE HERE

Notes: ....

GEAL CHARN

Region	Area	Height
Loch Treig to Loch Ericht	Highland	1049 M /3442 FEET

Date: .... Munro order: ....

Duration: .... Summit time: ....

Distance covered: .... Start time: ___:___   Finish time: ___:___

Companions: ....

....

Weather condition:

☐ ☀ ☐ ⛅ ☐ ☁ ☐ 🌧 ☐ ⛈ ☐ 🌨

Rating

Difficulty: ☆☆☆☆☆
Relish: ☆☆☆☆☆
Memories: ☆☆☆☆☆

Notes: ....

BEINN A' CHAORAINN

Region	Area	Height
Loch Lochy to Loch Laggan	Highland	1049.1 M / 3442 FEET

Date: ....

Munro order: ....

Duration: ....

Summit time: ....

Distance covered: ....

Start time: ___:___   Finish time: ___:___

Companions: ....
....
....

— Rating —

Difficulty: ☆ ☆ ☆ ☆ ☆

Relish: ☆ ☆ ☆ ☆ ☆

Memories: ☆ ☆ ☆ ☆ ☆

— Weather condition: —

☐ ☐ ☐ ☐ ☐ ☐

PICTURE HERE

Notes: ....
....

GLAS TULAICHEAN

Region	Area	Height
Pitlochry to Braemar & Blairgowrie	Perth and Kinross	1051 M / 3448 FEET

Date: .... Munro order: ....

Duration: .... Summit time: ....

Distance covered: .... Start time: ___:___   Finish time: ___:___

Companions: ....

....

Rating

Difficulty: ☆☆☆☆☆

Relish: ☆☆☆☆☆

Memories: ☆☆☆☆☆

Weather condition:
☐ ☀ ☐ ⛅ ☐ ☁ ☐ 🌧 ☐ ⛈ ☐ 🌨

Notes: ....

....

SGURR A' CHAORACHAIN

Region	Area	Height
Kyle of Lochalsh to Garve	Highland	1053 M /3455 FEET

Date: ....

Munro order: ....

Duration: ....

Summit time: ....

Distance covered: ....

Start time: ___:___   Finish time: ___:___

Companions: ....

....

Rating

Difficulty: ☆ ☆ ☆ ☆ ☆

Relish: ☆ ☆ ☆ ☆ ☆

Memories: ☆ ☆ ☆ ☆ ☆

Weather condition:
☀ ⛅ ☁ 🌧 ⛈ ❄

PICTURE HERE

Notes: ....
....

TOLL CREAGACH

Region	Area	Height
The Fannaichs	Highland	1054 M / 3458 FEET

Date: .... Munro order: ....

Duration: .... Summit time: ....

Distance covered: .... Start time: ___:___   Finish time: ___:___

Companions: ....

....

— Weather condition: —   — Rating —

☀ 🌤 🌥 🌧 ⛈ 🌨

Difficulty: ☆ ☆ ☆ ☆ ☆
Relish: ☆ ☆ ☆ ☆ ☆
Memories: ☆ ☆ ☆ ☆ ☆

Notes: ....
....

STOB POITE COIRE ARDAIR

Region	Area	Height
The Fannaichs	Highland	1054 M / 3458 FEET

Date: .... Munro order: ....

Duration: .... Summit time: ....

Distance covered: .... Start time: ___:___   Finish time: ___:___

Companions: ....

....

—— Weather condition: ——

—— Rating ——

Difficulty: ☆ ☆ ☆ ☆ ☆

Relish: ☆ ☆ ☆ ☆ ☆

Memories: ☆ ☆ ☆ ☆ ☆

PICTURE HERE

Notes: ....
....

NA GRUAGAICHEAN

Region	Area	Height
Fort William to Loch Treig & Loch Leven	Highland	1054.2 M / 3459 FEET

Date: ....

Munro order: ....

Duration: ....

Summit time: ....

Distance covered: ....

Start time: ___:___   Finish time: ___:___

Companions: ....
....

Rating
Difficulty: ☆☆☆☆☆
Relish: ☆☆☆☆☆
Memories: ☆☆☆☆☆

Weather condition: ☀ ⛅ 🌫 🌧 ⛈ 🌨

Notes: ....
....

LIATHACH
SPIDEAN A' CHOIRE LEITH

Region	Area	Height
Loch Torridon to Loch Maree	Highland	1054.8 M / 3461 FEET

Date: .... Munro order: ....

Duration: .... Summit time: ....

Distance covered: .... Start time: ___:___   Finish time: ___:___

Companions: ....

....

—— Weather condition: ——

☐ ☀️ ☐ ⛅ ☐ ☁️ ☐ 🌧️ ☐ ⛈️ ☐ 🌨️

—— Rating ——

Difficulty: ☆ ☆ ☆ ☆ ☆

Relish: ☆ ☆ ☆ ☆ ☆

Memories: ☆ ☆ ☆ ☆ ☆

PICTURE HERE

Notes: ....

....

AN TEALLACH
SGURR FIONA

Region	Area	Height
Loch Maree to Loch Broom	Highland	1058.6 M / 3473 FEET

Date: .... Munro order: ....

Duration: .... Summit time: ....

Distance covered: .... Start time: ___:___   Finish time: ___:___

Companions: ....

— Rating —

Difficulty: ☆☆☆☆☆

Relish: ☆☆☆☆☆

Memories: ☆☆☆☆☆

— Weather condition: —

☀ ⛅ ☁ 🌧 ⛈ ❄

Notes: ....

AN TEALLACH
BIDEIN A' GHLAS THUILL

Region	Area	Height
Loch Maree to Loch Broom	Highland	1062.5 M / 3486 FEET

Date: ....

Duration: ....

Distance covered: ....

Companions: ....
....
....

Munro order: ....

Summit time: ....

Start time: ___:___   Finish time: ___:___

— Rating —
Difficulty: ☆☆☆☆☆
Relish: ☆☆☆☆☆
Memories: ☆☆☆☆☆

— Weather condition: —
☀ 🌤 ☁ 🌧 ⛈ 🌨

Notes: ....
....

CAIRN OF CLAISE

Region	Area	Height
Braemar to Montrose	Aberdeenshire / Angus	1064 M / 3491 FEET

Date: .... Munro order: ....

Duration: .... Summit time: ....

Distance covered: .... Start time: ___:___   Finish time: ___:___

Companions: ....

....

Weather condition: ☀ ⛅ 🌬 🌧 ⛈ 🌨

Rating
- Difficulty: ☆☆☆☆☆
- Relish: ☆☆☆☆☆
- Memories: ☆☆☆☆☆

Notes: ....

GLAS MAOL

Region	Area	Height
Braemar to Montrose	Angus	1068 M /3504 FEET

Date: ....

Munro order: ....

Duration: ....

Summit time: ....

Distance covered: ....

Start time: ___:___   Finish time: ___:___

Companions: ....
....
....

— Weather condition: —
☀ ⛅ 🌥 🌧 ⛈ 🌨

— Rating —
Difficulty: ☆☆☆☆☆
Relish: ☆☆☆☆☆
Memories: ☆☆☆☆☆

PICTURE HERE

Notes: ....
....

SGURR FHUARAN

Region	Area	Height
Loch Arkaig to Glen Moriston	Highland	1068.7 M / 3506 FEET

Date: .... Munro order: ....

Duration: .... Summit time: ....

Distance covered: .... Start time: ___:___   Finish time: ___:___

Companions: ....

....

Rating

Difficulty: ☆☆☆☆☆

Relish: ☆☆☆☆☆

Memories: ☆☆☆☆☆

Weather condition:
☀ ⛅ ☁ 🌧 ⛈ 🌨

Notes: ....
....

AN SOCACH

Region	Area	Height
Killilan to Inverness	Highland	1069 M / 3507 FEET

Date: ....

Munro order: ....

Duration: ....

Summit time: ....

Distance covered: ....

Start time: ___:___   Finish time: ___:___

Companions: ....
....
....

Rating

Difficulty: ☆ ☆ ☆ ☆ ☆

Relish: ☆ ☆ ☆ ☆ ☆

Memories: ☆ ☆ ☆ ☆ ☆

Weather condition: ☐ ☀ ☐ ⛅ ☐ ☁ ☐ 🌧 ☐ ⛈ ☐ 🌨

Notes: ....
....

MEALL CORRANAICH

Region	Area	Height
Glen Lyon to Glen Dochart & Loch Tay	Perth and Kinross	1069 M /3507 FEET

Date: .... Munro order: ....

Duration: .... Summit time: ....

Distance covered: .... Start time: ___:___   Finish time: ___:___

Companions: ....
....

— Weather condition: —

☐ ☀ ☐ ⛅ ☐ 🌥 ☐ 🌧 ☐ ⛈ ☐ 🌨

— Rating —

Difficulty: ☆☆☆☆☆
Relish: ☆☆☆☆☆
Memories: ☆☆☆☆☆

Notes: ....
....

BEINN A' GHLO
BRAIGH COIRE CHRUINN-BHALGAIN

Region	Area	Height
Pitlochry to Braemar & Blairgowrie	Perth and Kinross	1070 M / 3510 FEET

Date: ....

Munro order: ....

Duration: ....

Summit time: ....

Distance covered: ....

Start time: ___:___   Finish time: ___:___

Companions: ....
....
....

— Rating —
Difficulty: ☆ ☆ ☆ ☆ ☆
Relish: ☆ ☆ ☆ ☆ ☆
Memories: ☆ ☆ ☆ ☆ ☆

— Weather condition: —
☐ ☀ ☐ ⛅ ☐ ☁ ☐ 🌧 ☐ ⛈ ☐ 🌨

PICTURE HERE

Notes: ....
....

BIDEAN NAM BIAN
STOB COIRE SGREAMHACH

Region	Area	Height
Loch Linnhe to Loch Etive	Highland	1072 M / 3517 FEET

Date: .... Munro order: ....

Duration: .... Summit time: ....

Distance covered: .... Start time: ___:___   Finish time: ___:___

Companions: ....
....
....

Weather condition: ☀ ⛅ ☁ 🌧 ⛈ 🌨

Rating
Difficulty: ☆☆☆☆☆
Relish: ☆☆☆☆☆
Memories: ☆☆☆☆☆

Notes: ....
....

BEINN DORAIN

Region	Area	Height
Loch Rannoch to Glen Lyon	Argyll and Bute	1076 M / 3530 FEET

Date: ....

Duration: ....

Distance covered: ....

Companions: ....
....
....

Munro order: ....

Summit time: ....

Start time: ___:___   Finish time: ___:___

Weather condition:
☐ ☀ ☐ ⛅ ☐ ☁ ☐ 🌧 ☐ ⛈ ☐ 🌨

Rating
Difficulty: ☆ ☆ ☆ ☆ ☆
Relish: ☆ ☆ ☆ ☆ ☆
Memories: ☆ ☆ ☆ ☆ ☆

PICTURE HERE

Notes: ....
....

BEINN HEASGARNICH

Region	Area	Height
Glen Lyon to Glen Dochart & Loch Tay	Perth and Kinross	1077.4 M /3535 FEET

Date: ....

Munro order: ....

Duration: ....

Summit time: ....

Distance covered: ....

Start time: ___:___   Finish time: ___:___

Companions: ....
....
....

Weather condition:

Rating

Difficulty: ☆☆☆☆☆

Relish: ☆☆☆☆☆

Memories: ☆☆☆☆☆

PICTURE HERE

Notes: ....
....

BEN STARAV

Region	Area	Height
Glen Etive to Glen Lochy	Highland	1079.5 M /3542 FEET

Date: .... Munro order: ....

Duration: .... Summit time: ....

Distance covered: .... Start time: ___:___   Finish time: ___:___

Companions: ....

....

—— Weather condition: ——

—— Rating ——

Difficulty: ☆☆☆☆☆

Relish: ☆☆☆☆☆

Memories: ☆☆☆☆☆

PICTURE HERE

Notes: ....

BEINN A' CHREACHAIN

Region	Area	Height
Loch Rannoch to Glen Lyon	Perth and Kinross	1080.6 M / 3545 FEET

Date: ....
Munro order: ....

Duration: ....
Summit time: ....

Distance covered: ....
Start time: ___:___   Finish time: ___:___

Companions: ....
....

— Weather condition: —
☐ ☀️ ☐ ⛅ ☐ 🌥️ ☐ 🌧️ ☐ ⛈️ ☐ 🌨️

— Rating —
Difficulty: ☆☆☆☆☆
Relish: ☆☆☆☆☆
Memories: ☆☆☆☆☆

PICTURE HERE

Notes: ....
....

SGURR A' CHOIRE GHLAIS

Region	Area	Height
Kyle of Lochalsh to Garve	Highland	1083 M / 3553 FEET

Date: .... Munro order: ....

Duration: .... Summit time: ....

Distance covered: .... Start time: ___:___   Finish time: ___:___

Companions: ....

....

— Weather condition: —

☀ ⛅ ☁ 🌧 ⛈ ❄

— Rating —

Difficulty: ☆ ☆ ☆ ☆ ☆

Relish: ☆ ☆ ☆ ☆ ☆

Memories: ☆ ☆ ☆ ☆ ☆

PICTURE HERE

Notes: ....

....

BEINN A' CHAORAINN

Region	Area	Height
Cairngorms	Aberdeenshire /Moray	1083 M /3553 FEET

Date: .... Munro order: ....

Duration: .... Summit time: ....

Distance covered: .... Start time: ___:___   Finish time: ___:___

Companions: ....
....
....

Weather condition:
☀ ⛅ ☁ 🌧 ⛈ 🌨

Rating
Difficulty: ☆☆☆☆☆
Relish: ☆☆☆☆☆
Memories: ☆☆☆☆☆

Notes: ....
....

SCHIEHALLION

Region	Area	Height
Loch Rannoch to Glen Lyon	Perth and Kinross	1083 M / 3553 FEET

Date: ....

Duration: ....

Distance covered: ....

Munro order: ....

Summit time: ....

Start time: ___:___   Finish time: ___:___

Companions: ....
....

Weather condition:

Rating

Difficulty: ☆☆☆☆☆

Relish: ☆☆☆☆☆

Memories: ☆☆☆☆☆

PICTURE HERE

Notes: ....
....

BEINN DEARG

Region	Area	Height
Loch Broom to Strath Oykel	Highland	1084 M /3556 FEET

Date: .... Munro order: ....

Duration: .... Summit time: ....

Distance covered: .... Start time: ___:___   Finish time: ___:___

Companions: ....
....
....

— Weather condition: —   — Rating —

☀️ ⛅ 🌥️ 🌧️ ⛈️ 🌨️

Difficulty: ☆☆☆☆☆
Relish: ☆☆☆☆☆
Memories: ☆☆☆☆☆

[PICTURE HERE]

Notes: ....
....

BEINN A' CHLACHAIR

Region	Area	Height
Loch Treig to Loch Ericht	Highland	1087 M / 3566 FEET

Date: ....

Munro order: ....

Duration: ....

Summit time: ....

Distance covered: ....

Start time: ___:___   Finish time: ___:___

Companions: ....
....

— Weather condition: —

— Rating —

Difficulty: ☆☆☆☆☆

Relish: ☆☆☆☆☆

Memories: ☆☆☆☆☆

Notes: ....
....

BYNACK MORE

Region	Area	Height
Cairngorms	Highland	1090 M /3576 FEET

Date: .... Munro order: ....

Duration: .... Summit time: ....

Distance covered: .... Start time: ___:___   Finish time: ___:___

Companions: ....
....
....

— Weather condition: —
☀ ⛅ ☁ 🌧 ⛈ 🌨

— Rating —
Difficulty: ☆☆☆☆☆
Relish: ☆☆☆☆☆
Memories: ☆☆☆☆☆

Notes: ....
....

STOB GHABHAR

Region	Area	Height
Loch Arkaig to Glen Moriston	Highland	1090 M /3576 FEET

Date: ....

Duration: ....

Distance covered: ....

Companions: ....
....
....

Munro order: ....

Summit time: ....

Start time: ___:___   Finish time: ___:___

Rating

Difficulty: ☆ ☆ ☆ ☆ ☆

Relish: ☆ ☆ ☆ ☆ ☆

Memories: ☆ ☆ ☆ ☆ ☆

Weather condition:
☐ ☀ ☐ ⛅ ☐ ☁ ☐ 🌧 ☐ ⛈ ☐ ❄

Notes: ....
....

SGURR NAN CLACH GEALA

Region	Area	Height
Loch Rannoch to Glen Lyon	Perth and Kinross	1093 M / 3586 FEET

Date: .... Munro order: ....

Duration: .... Summit time: ....

Distance covered: .... Start time: ___:___   Finish time: ___:___

Companions: ....
....
....

— Weather condition: —

— Rating —

Difficulty: ☆☆☆☆☆
Relish: ☆☆☆☆☆
Memories: ☆☆☆☆☆

Notes: ....
....

SGURR CHOINNICH MOR

Region	Area	Height
Loch Rannoch to Glen Lyon	Perth and Kinross	1094 M /3589 FEET

Date: ....

Duration: ....

Distance covered: ....

Companions: ....
....
....

Munro order: ....

Summit time: ....

Start time: ___:___   Finish time: ___:___

— Weather condition: —
☐ ☀ ☐ ⛅ ☐ ☁ ☐ 🌧 ☐ ⛈ ☐ 🌨

— Rating —
Difficulty: ☆☆☆☆☆
Relish: ☆☆☆☆☆
Memories: ☆☆☆☆☆

PICTURE HERE

Notes: ....
....

SGURR A' MHAIM

Region	Area	Height
Fort William to Loch Treig & Loch Leven	Highland	1099 M /3606 FEET

Date: .... Munro order: ....

Duration: .... Summit time: ....

Distance covered: .... Start time: ___:___   Finish time: ___:___

Companions: ....
....
....

Weather condition:
☀ ⛅ ☁ 🌧 ⛈ 🌨

Rating
Difficulty: ☆☆☆☆☆
Relish: ☆☆☆☆☆
Memories: ☆☆☆☆☆

Notes: ....
....

CREISE

Region	Area	Height
Glen Etive to Glen Lochy	Highland	1099.8 M /3608 FEET

Date: ....

Munro order: ....

Duration: ....

Summit time: ....

Distance covered: ....

Start time: ___:___   Finish time: ___:___

Companions: ....

....

....

— Weather condition: —

— Rating —

Difficulty: ☆ ☆ ☆ ☆ ☆

Relish: ☆ ☆ ☆ ☆ ☆

Memories: ☆ ☆ ☆ ☆ ☆

Notes: ....

....

MULLACH FRAOCH-CHOIRE

Region	Area	Height
Glen Affric to Glen Moriston	Highland	1102 M / 3615 FEET

Date: .... Munro order: ....

Duration: .... Summit time: ....

Distance covered: .... Start time: ___:___   Finish time: ___:___

Companions: ....

....

— Weather condition: —

☀️ ⛅ 🌥️ 🌧️ ⛈️ 🌨️

— Rating —

Difficulty: ☆☆☆☆☆
Relish: ☆☆☆☆☆
Memories: ☆☆☆☆☆

Notes: ....

BEINN GHLAS

Region	Area	Height
Glen Lyon to Glen Dochart & Loch Tay	Perth and Kinross	1103 M / 3619 FEET

Date: ....

Munro order: ....

Duration: ....

Summit time: ....

Distance covered: ....

Start time: ___:___   Finish time: ___:___

Companions: ....

....

— Rating —

Difficulty: ☆ ☆ ☆ ☆ ☆

— Weather condition: —

Relish: ☆ ☆ ☆ ☆ ☆

Memories: ☆ ☆ ☆ ☆ ☆

PICTURE HERE

Notes: ....

BEINN EIBHINN

Region	Area	Height
Loch Treig to Loch Ericht	Highland	1103.2 M / 3619 FEET

Date: .... Munro order: ....

Duration: .... Summit time: ....

Distance covered: .... Start time: ___:___   Finish time: ___:___

Companions: ....

....

—— Weather condition: ——

☀ ⛅ 🌥 🌧 ⛈ 🌨

—— Rating ——

Difficulty: ☆☆☆☆☆

Relish: ☆☆☆☆☆

Memories: ☆☆☆☆☆

Notes: ....

....

STOB A' CHOIRE MHEADHOIN

Region	Area	Height
Loch Arkaig to Glen Moriston	Highland	1105 M / 3625 FEET

Date: ....

Munro order: ....

Duration: ....

Summit time: ....

Distance covered: ....

Start time: ___:___   Finish time: ___:___

Companions: ....
....

— Rating —

Difficulty: ☆ ☆ ☆ ☆ ☆

Relish: ☆ ☆ ☆ ☆ ☆

Memories: ☆ ☆ ☆ ☆ ☆

— Weather condition: —

☐ ☐ ☐ ☐ ☐ ☐

PICTURE HERE

Notes: ....
....

MEALL A' BHUIRIDH

Region	Area	Height
Glen Etive to Glen Lochy	Highland	1107.9 M /3635 FEET

Date: .... Munro order: ....

Duration: .... Summit time: ....

Distance covered: .... Start time: ___:___   Finish time: ___:___

Companions: ....

....

....

Weather condition:

☐ ☀ ☐ ⛅ ☐ ☁ ☐ 🌧 ☐ ⛈ ☐ 🌨

Rating
- Difficulty: ☆☆☆☆☆
- Relish: ☆☆☆☆☆
- Memories: ☆☆☆☆☆

PICTURE HERE

Notes: ....

....

SGURR NAN COIREACHAN

Region	Area	Height
Loch Arkaig to Glen Moriston	Highland	956 M / 3136 FEET

Date: .... Munro order: ....

Duration: .... Summit time: ....

Distance covered: .... Start time: ___:___   Finish time: ___:___

Companions: ....
....

— Weather condition: —

☐ ☀ ☐ ⛅ ☐ ☁ ☐ 🌧 ☐ ⛈ ☐ 🌨

— Rating —

Difficulty: ☆ ☆ ☆ ☆ ☆

Relish: ☆ ☆ ☆ ☆ ☆

Memories: ☆ ☆ ☆ ☆ ☆

PICTURE HERE

Notes: ....
....

SGURR MOR

Region	Area	Height
Loch Rannoch to Glen Lyon	Perth and Kinross	1109 M / 3638 FEET

Date: .... Munro order: ....

Duration: .... Summit time: ....

Distance covered: .... Start time: ___:___   Finish time: ___:___

Companions: ....

....

— Weather condition: —

☀️ ⛅ 🌥️ 🌧️ ⛈️ 🌨️

— Rating —

Difficulty: ☆☆☆☆☆
Relish: ☆☆☆☆☆
Memories: ☆☆☆☆☆

Notes: ....

CAIRN A' CHOIRE BHOIDHEACH

Region	Area	Height
Braemar to Montrose	Aberdeenshire	1109.9 M /3641 FEET

Date: ....

Duration: ....

Distance covered: ....

Companions: ....
....
....

Weather condition:
☐ ☀ ☐ ⛅ ☐ ☁ ☐ 🌧 ☐ ⛈ ☐ 🌨

Munro order: ....

Summit time: ....

Start time: ___:___   Finish time: ___:___

Rating
Difficulty: ☆ ☆ ☆ ☆ ☆
Relish: ☆ ☆ ☆ ☆ ☆
Memories: ☆ ☆ ☆ ☆ ☆

PICTURE HERE

Notes: ....
....

TOM A' CHOINICH

Region	Area	Height
The Fannaichs	Highland	1112 M / 3648 FEET

Date: .... Munro order: ....

Duration: .... Summit time: ....

Distance covered: .... Start time: ___:___   Finish time: ___:___

Companions: ....

....

Weather condition:
☐ ☀️ ☐ ⛅ ☐ 🌥️ ☐ 🌧️ ☐ ⛈️ ☐ 🌨️

Rating
Difficulty: ☆☆☆☆☆
Relish: ☆☆☆☆☆
Memories: ☆☆☆☆☆

Notes: ....
....

MONADH MOR

Region	Area	Height
Cairngorms	Aberdeenshire/ Highland	1113 M /3652 FEET

Date: .... Munro order: ....

Duration: .... Summit time: ....

Distance covered: .... Start time: ___:___   Finish time: ___:___

Companions: ....

— Rating —

Difficulty: ☆☆☆☆☆

Relish: ☆☆☆☆☆

Memories: ☆☆☆☆☆

— Weather condition: —
☐ ☀ ☐ ⛅ ☐ 🌥 ☐ 🌧 ☐ ⛈ ☐ 🌨

Notes: ....
....

STOB COIRE EASAIN

Region	Area	Height
The Fannaichs	Highland	1115 M / 3658 FEET

Date: .... Munro order: ....

Duration: .... Summit time: ....

Distance covered: .... Start time: ___:___   Finish time: ___:___

Companions: ....
....

Weather condition:
☐ ☀ ☐ ⛅ ☐ ☁ ☐ 🌧 ☐ ⛈ ☐ 🌨

Rating
Difficulty: ☆☆☆☆☆
Relish: ☆☆☆☆☆
Memories: ☆☆☆☆☆

Notes: ....
....

AONACH BEAG

Region	Area	Height
Loch Treig to Loch Ericht	Highland	1115.8 M / 3661 FEET

Date: .... Munro order: ....

Duration: .... Summit time: ....

Distance covered: .... Start time: ___:___   Finish time: ___:___

Companions: ....
....

— Weather condition: —

☀ ⛅ ☁ 🌧 ⛈ 🌨

— Rating —

Difficulty: ☆☆☆☆☆

Relish: ☆☆☆☆☆

Memories: ☆☆☆☆☆

PICTURE HERE

Notes: ....
....

STOB COIRE AN LAOIGH

Region	Area	Height
Loch Arkaig to Glen Moriston	Highland	1116 M / 3661 FEET

Date: .... Munro order: ....

Duration: .... Summit time: ....

Distance covered: .... Start time: ___:___   Finish time: ___:___

Companions: ....
....

Weather condition:
☐ ☀ ☐ ⛅ ☐ 🌥 ☐ 🌧 ☐ ⛈ ☐ 🌨

Rating
Difficulty: ☆☆☆☆☆
Relish: ☆☆☆☆☆
Memories: ☆☆☆☆☆

Notes: ....
....

AN STUC

Region	Area	Height
Glen Lyon to Glen Dochart & Loch Tay	Perth and Kinross	1117.1 M / 3665 FEET

Date: .... Munro order: ....

Duration: .... Summit time: ....

Distance covered: .... Start time: ___:___   Finish time: ___:___

Companions: ....

....

— Weather condition: —

☐ ☀ ☐ ⛅ ☐ ☁ ☐ 🌧 ☐ ⛈ ☐ 🌨

— Rating —

Difficulty: ☆☆☆☆☆

Relish: ☆☆☆☆☆

Memories: ☆☆☆☆☆

PICTURE HERE

Notes: ....
....

SGOR GAOITH

Region	Area	Height
Cairngorms	Highland	1118 M / 3668 FEET

Date: .... Munro order: ....

Duration: .... Summit time: ....

Distance covered: .... Start time: ___:___ Finish time: ___:___

Companions: ....
....

— Weather condition: — ☐ ☀ ☐ ⛅ ☐ 🌫 ☐ 🌧 ☐ ⛈ ☐ 🌨

— Rating —
Difficulty: ☆☆☆☆☆
Relish: ☆☆☆☆☆
Memories: ☆☆☆☆☆

Notes: ....
....

A' CHRAILEAG

Region	Area	Height
Glen Affric to Glen Moriston	Highland	1120 M / 3675 FEET

Date: .... Munro order: ....

Duration: .... Summit time: ....

Distance covered: .... Start time: ___:___   Finish time: ___:___

Companions: ....

....

─── Weather condition: ───

─── Rating ───

Difficulty: ☆☆☆☆☆

Relish: ☆☆☆☆☆

Memories: ☆☆☆☆☆

PICTURE HERE

Notes: ....
....

BEINN A' GHLO
CARN NAN GABHAR

Region	Area	Height
Pitlochry to Braemar & Blairgowrie	Perth and Kinross	1121.9 M /3681 FEET

Date: .... Munro order: ....

Duration: .... Summit time: ....

Distance covered: .... Start time: __:__   Finish time: __:__

Companions: ....
....
....

Weather condition:
☀ ⛅ ☁ 🌧 ⛈ 🌨

Rating
Difficulty: ☆☆☆☆☆
Relish: ☆☆☆☆☆
Memories: ☆☆☆☆☆

Notes: ....
....

250

MEALL GARBH

Region	Area	Height
Glen Lyon to Glen Dochart & Loch Tay	Perth and Kinross	1123.1 M / 3685 FEET

Date: .... Munro order: ....

Duration: .... Summit time: ....

Distance covered: .... Start time: ___:___   Finish time: ___:___

Companions: ....

....

----- Weather condition: -----

☀ ⛅ ☁ 🌧 ⛈ ❄

----- Rating -----

Difficulty: ☆☆☆☆☆

Relish: ☆☆☆☆☆

Memories: ☆☆☆☆☆

Notes: ....

BEN CRUACHAN

Region	Area	Height
Glen Etive to Glen Lochy	Argyll and Bute	1,127 M /3698 FEET

Date: .... Munro order: ....

Duration: .... Summit time: ....

Distance covered: .... Start time: ___:___   Finish time: ___:___

Companions: ....
....

Weather condition:
☀️ ⛅ 🌥️ 🌧️ ⛈️ 🌨️

Rating
Difficulty: ☆☆☆☆☆
Relish: ☆☆☆☆☆
Memories: ☆☆☆☆☆

PICTURE HERE

Notes: ....
....

CREAG MEAGAIDH

Region	Area	Height
Loch Lochy to Loch Laggan	Highland	1128 M / 3701 FEET

Date: ....

Duration: ....

Distance covered: ....

Companions: ....
....
....

Weather condition:
☐ ☀ ☐ ⛅ ☐ ☁ ☐ 🌧 ☐ ⛈ ☐ 🌨

Munro order: ....

Summit time: ....

Start time: ___:___   Finish time: ___:___

Rating

Difficulty: ☆ ☆ ☆ ☆ ☆

Relish: ☆ ☆ ☆ ☆ ☆

Memories: ☆ ☆ ☆ ☆ ☆

Notes: ....
....

AN RIABHACHAN

Region	Area	Height
Killilan to Inverness	Highland	923.9 M /3704 FEET

Date: .... Munro order: ....

Duration: .... Summit time: ....

Distance covered: .... Start time: ___:___   Finish time: ___:___

Companions: ....

— Rating —
Difficulty: ☆☆☆☆☆
Relish: ☆☆☆☆☆
Memories: ☆☆☆☆☆

— Weather condition: —
☀ ⛅ 🌫 🌧 ⛈ 🌨

Notes: ....

BINNEIN MOR

Region	Area	Height
Fort Wiliam to Loch Treig & Loch Leven	Highland	1130 M /3707 FEET

Date: ....

Munro order: ....

Duration: ....

Summit time: ....

Distance covered: ....

Start time: ___:___   Finish time: ___:___

Companions: ....
....

Rating
Difficulty: ☆ ☆ ☆ ☆ ☆
Relish: ☆ ☆ ☆ ☆ ☆
Memories: ☆ ☆ ☆ ☆ ☆

Weather condition:
☐ ☀ ☐ ⛅ ☐ ☁ ☐ 🌧 ☐ ⛈ ☐ 🌨

PICTURE HERE

Notes: ....
....

BEN LUI

Region	Area	Height
Inveraray to Crianlarich	Stirling	1130 M / 3707 FEET

Date: .... Munro order: ....

Duration: .... Summit time: ....

Distance covered: .... Start time: ___:___   Finish time: ___:___

Companions: ....
....

Weather condition: ☀ ⛅ 🌥 🌧 ⛈ 🌨

Rating
Difficulty: ☆☆☆☆☆
Relish: ☆☆☆☆☆
Memories: ☆☆☆☆☆

PICTURE HERE

Notes: ....
....

GEAL-CHARN

Region	Area	Height
Loch Treig to Loch Ericht	Highland	1132 M / 3714 FEET

Date: ....   Munro order: ....

Duration: ....   Summit time: ....

Distance covered: ....   Start time: ___:___   Finish time: ___:___

Companions: ....

....

— Weather condition: —   — Rating —

☀ ⛅ ☁ 🌧 ⛈ 🌨   Difficulty: ☆☆☆☆☆
                  Relish: ☆☆☆☆☆
                  Memories: ☆☆☆☆☆

PICTURE HERE

Notes: ....

....

BEN ALDER

Region	Area	Height
Loch Treig to Loch Ericht	Highland	1148 M / 3766 FEET

Date: .... Munro order: ....

Duration: .... Summit time: ....

Distance covered: .... Start time: ___:___   Finish time: ___:___

Companions: ....

....

── Weather condition: ──

☀ ⛅ 🌫 🌧 ⛈ 🌨

── Rating ──

Difficulty: ☆ ☆ ☆ ☆ ☆

Relish: ☆ ☆ ☆ ☆ ☆

Memories: ☆ ☆ ☆ ☆ ☆

Notes: ....

....

BIDEAN NAM BIAN

Region	Area	Height
Loch Linnhe to Loch Etive	Highland	1149.4 M /3771 FEET

Date: ....

Munro order: ....

Duration: ....

Summit time: ....

Distance covered: ....

Start time: ___:___   Finish time: ___:___

Companions: ....
....
....

— Weather condition: —
☀ ⛅ ☁ 🌧 ⛈ 🌨

— Rating —

Difficulty: ☆ ☆ ☆ ☆ ☆

Relish: ☆ ☆ ☆ ☆ ☆

Memories: ☆ ☆ ☆ ☆ ☆

PICTURE HERE

Notes: ....
....

SGURR NA LAPAICH

Region	Area	Height
Loch Rannoch to Glen Lyon	Perth and Kinross	1151 M / 3776 FEET

Date: .... Munro order: ....

Duration: .... Summit time: ....

Distance covered: .... Start time: ___:___   Finish time: ___:___

Companions: ....

....

Weather condition:

☐ ☀ ☐ ⛅ ☐ ☁ ☐ 🌧 ☐ ⛈ ☐ 🌨

Rating
Difficulty: ☆☆☆☆☆
Relish: ☆☆☆☆☆
Memories: ☆☆☆☆☆

Notes: ....

....

SGURR NAN CEATHREAMHNAN

Region	Area	Height
Loch Arkaig to Glen Moriston	Highland	1151 M / 3776 FEET

Date: ....

Munro order: ....

Duration: ....

Summit time: ....

Distance covered: ....

Start time: ___:___   Finish time: ___:___

Companions: ....
....

Rating

Difficulty: ☆☆☆☆☆
Relish: ☆☆☆☆☆
Memories: ☆☆☆☆☆

Weather condition:
☀ ⛅ ☁ 🌧 ⛈ 🌨

Notes: ....
....

DERRY CAIRNGORM

Region	Area	Height
Cairngorms	Aberdeenshire	1155 M / 3789 FEET

Date: .... Munro order: ....

Duration: .... Summit time: ....

Distance covered: .... Start time: ___:___   Finish time: ___:___

Companions: ....

— Weather condition: —

— Rating —

Difficulty: ☆☆☆☆☆
Relish: ☆☆☆☆☆
Memories: ☆☆☆☆☆

Notes: ....

LOCHNAGAR

Region	Area	Height
Braemar to Montrose	Aberdeenshire	1155.7 M / 3792 FEET

Date: .... Munro order: ....

Duration: .... Summit time: ....

Distance covered: .... Start time: ___:___ Finish time: ___:___

Companions: ....
....

Weather condition: ☀ ⛅ 🌥 🌧 ⛈ 🌨

Rating
Difficulty: ☆☆☆☆☆
Relish: ☆☆☆☆☆
Memories: ☆☆☆☆☆

PICTURE HERE

Notes: ....
....

BEINN BHROTAIN

Region	Area	Height
Cairngorms	Aberdeenshire	1157 M / 3796 FEET

Date: .... Munro order: ....

Duration: .... Summit time: ....

Distance covered: .... Start time: ___:___   Finish time: ___:___

Companions: ....

....

— Weather condition: —

☐ ☀   ☐ ⛅   ☐ ☁   ☐ 🌧   ☐ ⛈   ☐ 🌨

— Rating —

Difficulty: ☆ ☆ ☆ ☆ ☆

Relish: ☆ ☆ ☆ ☆ ☆

Memories: ☆ ☆ ☆ ☆ ☆

PICTURE HERE

Notes: ....

....

STOB BINNEIN

Region	Area	Height
Loch Arkaig to Glen Moriston	Highland	1165 M / 3822 FEET

Date: ....

Munro order: ....

Duration: ....

Summit time: ....

Distance covered: ....

Start time: ____:____   Finish time: ____:____

Companions: ....
....
....

— Weather condition —
☀ 🌤 ☁ 🌧 ⛈ 🌨

— Rating —
Difficulty: ☆ ☆ ☆ ☆ ☆
Relish: ☆ ☆ ☆ ☆ ☆
Memories: ☆ ☆ ☆ ☆ ☆

PICTURE HERE

Notes: ....
....

BEN AVON

Region	Area	Height
Cairngorms	Aberdeeshire /Moray	1171 M /3842 FEET

Date: .... Munro order: ....

Duration: .... Summit time: ....

Distance covered: .... Start time: ___:___   Finish time: ___:___

Companions: ....

....

— Weather condition: —   — Rating —

☀️ ⛅ ☁️ 🌧️ ⛈️ 🌨️

Difficulty: ☆☆☆☆☆
Relish: ☆☆☆☆☆
Memories: ☆☆☆☆☆

Notes: ....

....

BEN MORE

Region	Area	Height
Loch Lomond to Strathyre	Stirling	1174 M / 3852 FEET

Date: .... Munro order: ....

Duration: .... Summit time: ....

Distance covered: .... Start time: ___:___   Finish time: ___:___

Companions: ....
....

Weather condition: ☀ ⛅ ☁ 🌧 ⛈ 🌨

Rating
Difficulty: ☆☆☆☆☆
Relish: ☆☆☆☆☆
Memories: ☆☆☆☆☆

PICTURE HERE

Notes: ....
....

STOB CHOIRE CLAURIGH

Region	Area	Height
The Fannaichs	Highland	1177 M /3862 FEET

Date: .... Munro order: ....

Duration: .... Summit time: ....

Distance covered: .... Start time: ___:___   Finish time: ___:___

Companions: ....

....

— Weather condition: —

☐ ☀ ☐ ⛅ ☐ 🌥 ☐ 🌧 ☐ ⛈ ☐ 🌨

— Rating —

Difficulty: ☆☆☆☆☆
Relish: ☆☆☆☆☆
Memories: ☆☆☆☆☆

Notes: ....

....

MAM SODHAIL

Region	Area	Height
Loch Duich to Cannich	Highland	1179.4 M /3869 FEET

Date: ....

Duration: ....

Distance covered: ....

Companions: ....
....
....

Munro order: ....

Summit time: ....

Start time: ___:___   Finish time: ___:___

— Weather condition: —
☀ ⛅ 🌫 🌧 ⛈ 🌨

— Rating —
Difficulty: ☆☆☆☆☆
Relish: ☆☆☆☆☆
Memories: ☆☆☆☆☆

PICTURE HERE

Notes: ....
....

CARN EIGE

Region	Area	Height
Loch Duich to Cannich	Highland	1182.8 M /3881 FEET

Date: ....

Duration: ....

Distance covered: ....

Companions: ....
....

Munro order: ....

Summit time: ....

Start time: ___:___   Finish time: ___:___

— Rating —

Difficulty: ☆ ☆ ☆ ☆ ☆

Relish: ☆ ☆ ☆ ☆ ☆

Memories: ☆ ☆ ☆ ☆ ☆

— Weather condition: —

☐ ☐ ☐ ☐ ☐
☀ ⛅ 🌥 🌧 ⛈ 🌨

PICTURE HERE

Notes: ....
....

BEINN MHEADHOIN

Region	Area	Height
Cairngorms	Moray	1182.9 M / 3881 FEET

Date: .... Munro order: ....

Duration: .... Summit time: ....

Distance covered: .... Start time: ___:___   Finish time: ___:___

Companions: ....
....
....

Weather condition:
☐ ☀ ☐ ⛅ ☐ ☁ ☐ 🌧 ☐ ⛈ ☐ 🌨

Rating
Difficulty: ☆ ☆ ☆ ☆ ☆
Relish: ☆ ☆ ☆ ☆ ☆
Memories: ☆ ☆ ☆ ☆ ☆

PICTURE HERE

Notes: ....
....

BEINN A' BHUIRD

Region	Area	Height
Cairngorms	Aberdeenshire /Moray	1197 M /3927 FEET

Date: .... Munro order: ....

Duration: .... Summit time: ....

Distance covered: .... Start time: ___:___   Finish time: ___:___

Companions: ....

....

— Weather condition: — ☐ ☀ ☐ 🌤 ☐ ☁ ☐ 🌧 ☐ ⛈ ☐ 🌨

— Rating —
Difficulty: ☆☆☆☆☆
Relish: ☆☆☆☆☆
Memories: ☆☆☆☆☆

Notes: ....

....

BEN LAWERS

Region	Area	Height
Glen Lyon to Glen Dochart & Loch Tay	Perth and Kinross	1214 M / 3983 FEET

Date: ....

Duration: ....

Distance covered: ....

Companions: ....
....
....

Munro order: ....

Summit time: ....

Start time: ___:___   Finish time: ___:___

Weather condition:
☐ ☀ ☐ ⛅ ☐ ☁ ☐ 🌧 ☐ ⛈ ☐ 🌨

Rating
Difficulty: ☆ ☆ ☆ ☆ ☆
Relish: ☆ ☆ ☆ ☆ ☆
Memories: ☆ ☆ ☆ ☆ ☆

Notes: ....
....

CARN MOR DEARG

Region	Area	Height
Fort William to Loch Treig & Loch Leven	Highland	1220 M / 4003 FEET

Date: .... Munro order: ....

Duration: .... Summit time: ....

Distance covered: .... Start time: ___:___   Finish time: ___:___

Companions: ....
....

Rating
Difficulty: ☆☆☆☆☆
Relish: ☆☆☆☆☆
Memories: ☆☆☆☆☆

Weather condition:
☐ ☀️ ☐ ⛅ ☐ 🌥️ ☐ 🌧️ ☐ ⛈️ ☐ 🌨️

PICTURE HERE

Notes: ....
....

AONACH MOR

Region	Area	Height
Fort William to Loch Treig & Loch Leven	Highland	1220.4 M / 4004 FEET

Date: ....

Duration: ....

Distance covered: ....

Companions: ....
....
....

Munro order: ....

Summit time: ....

Start time: ___:___ Finish time: ___:___

Rating

Difficulty: ☆ ☆ ☆ ☆ ☆

Relish: ☆ ☆ ☆ ☆ ☆

Memories: ☆ ☆ ☆ ☆ ☆

Weather condition: ☀ ⛅ ☁ 🌧 ⛈ 🌨

Notes: ....
....

AONACH BEAG

Region	Area	Height
Fort Wiliam to Loch Treig & Loch Leven	Highland	1234 M / 4049 FEET

Date: .... Munro order: ....

Duration: .... Summit time: ....

Distance covered: .... Start time: ___:___   Finish time: ___:___

Companions: ....
....

──── Weather condition: ────

☐ ☀   ☐ ⛅   ☐ 🌊☁   ☐ 🌧   ☐ 🌩   ☐ 🌨

──── Rating ────

Difficulty: ☆ ☆ ☆ ☆ ☆

Relish: ☆ ☆ ☆ ☆ ☆

Memories: ☆ ☆ ☆ ☆ ☆

Notes: ....
....

CAIRN GORM

Region	Area	Height
Cairngorms	Highland /Moray	1244.8 M /4084 FEET

Date: ....

Duration: ....

Distance covered: ....

Companions: ....
....
....

Munro order: ....

Summit time: ....

Start time: ____:____   Finish time: ____:____

───── Rating ─────

Difficulty: ☆ ☆ ☆ ☆ ☆

Relish: ☆ ☆ ☆ ☆ ☆

Memories: ☆ ☆ ☆ ☆ ☆

─── Weather condition: ───
☀ ⛅ ☁ 🌧 ⛈ 🌨

PICTURE HERE

Notes: ....
....

SGOR AN LOCHAIN UAINE

Region	Area	Height
Cairngorms	Aberdeenshire	1258 M /4127 FEET

Date: .... Munro order: ....

Duration: .... Summit time: ....

Distance covered: .... Start time: ___:___ Finish time: ___:___

Companions: ....

....

— Weather condition: — Rating

Difficulty: ☆☆☆☆☆
Relish: ☆☆☆☆☆
Memories: ☆☆☆☆☆

☐ ☀ ☐ ⛅ ☐ 🌥 ☐ 🌧 ☐ ⛈ ☐ 🌨

PICTURE HERE

Notes: ....
....

CAIRN TOUL

Region	Area	Height
Cairngorms	Aberdeenshire	1291 M / 4236 FEET

Date: .... Munro order: ....

Duration: .... Summit time: ....

Distance covered: .... Start time: ___:___   Finish time: ___:___

Companions: ....

....

—— Weather condition: ——

☐ ☀ ☐ ⛅ ☐ ☁ ☐ 🌧 ☐ ⛈ ☐ 🌨

—— Rating ——

Difficulty: ☆ ☆ ☆ ☆ ☆

Relish: ☆ ☆ ☆ ☆ ☆

Memories: ☆ ☆ ☆ ☆ ☆

PICTURE HERE

Notes: ....
....

BRAERIACH

Region	Area	Height
Cairngorms	Aberdeeshire /Highland	1296 M /4252 FEET

Date: .... Munro order: ....

Duration: .... Summit time: ....

Distance covered: .... Start time: ___:___   Finish time: ___:___

Companions: ....
....
....

Weather condition:
☀️ ⛅ 🌥️ 🌧️ ⛈️ 🌨️

Rating
Difficulty: ☆☆☆☆☆
Relish: ☆☆☆☆☆
Memories: ☆☆☆☆☆

Notes: ....
....

BEN MACDUI

Region	Area	Height
Cairngorms	Aberdeeshire /Moray	1309 M /4295 FEET

Date: .... Munro order: ....

Duration: .... Summit time: ....

Distance covered: .... Start time: ___:___   Finish time: ___:___

Companions: ....

....

— Weather condition: —

☐ ☀ ☐ ⛅ ☐ ☁ ☐ 🌧 ☐ ⛈ ☐ 🌨

— Rating —

Difficulty: ☆ ☆ ☆ ☆ ☆

Relish: ☆ ☆ ☆ ☆ ☆

Memories: ☆ ☆ ☆ ☆ ☆

PICTURE HERE

Notes: ....
....

BEN NEVIS

Region	Area	Height
Fort William to Loch Treig & Loch Leven	Highland	1344.527 M / 4411.18 FEET

Date: .... Munro order: ....

Duration: .... Summit time: ....

Distance covered: .... Start time: ___:___   Finish time: ___:___

Companions: ....

....

....

Weather condition: ☀ ⛅ 🌥 🌧 ⛈ 🌨

Rating
Difficulty: ☆☆☆☆☆
Relish: ☆☆☆☆☆
Memories: ☆☆☆☆☆

PICTURE HERE

Notes: ....
....

We hope that you found this logbook helpful in your Munros journey
If you like it, we will be happy to know your review.

Thank you !

Printed in Great Britain
by Amazon